TROPICAL FISH

There are few things indoors that will attract more attention than a well set up, electrically lit Tropical Aquarium. A collection of colourful fish, silently swimming in crystal clear water, against a background of rocks and growing green plants, forms a living picture that is both beautiful and of absorbing interest. In this little book the author, who owns one of the leading Tropical Fish Hatcheries in the country, McLynn's Aquarium, Ewhurst, Surrey, explains simply in easy stages the setting up, and maintenance of such an Aquarium. If followed closely, the information given will enable anyone to keep an Aquarium clean and clear indefinitely, with the minimum of cost, time and work.

General Editor: CHRISTINA FOYLE

The cover photograph shows Mottled Catfish, *Corydoras paleatus*

Foyle's Handbooks for pet lovers

TROPICAL FISH

Derek McInerny

W. & G. FOYLE LTD.
119-125 CHARING CROSS ROAD
LONDON, W.C.2

First published 1962
Reprinted 1963
Reprinted 1964
Reprinted 1965
Reprinted 1966

© *W. & G. Foyle Ltd. 1962*

Printed in Great Britain by
Northumberland Press Limited
Gateshead on Tyne

Contents

List of Illustrations

Introduction

THE BRITISH are celebrated for their love of Nature, and especially animals, whether four-legged, two-winged or fish-tailed.

But alas! with life as high-powered as it is today many of us just do not have the time to look after pets as we would wish. Many of us live in ever-expanding towns, perhaps in huge blocks of flats, with no garden or facilities for keeping dogs or cats. Some of us hardly ever see a blade of grass or a tree in full foliage, and yearn for a soothing sight of Nature.

It is no wonder, then, that the Tropical Aquarium continues to grow in popularity. Even where there are restrictions on the keeping of pets on grounds of noise or hygiene, a self-contained Aquarium is silent and clean. The fish do not have to be taken out for exercise, or to do their daily duties; they do not require special smelly foods to be cooked, nor do they need grooming. Even when going on holiday they can be safely left without food for up to a fortnight without harm.

An Aquarium properly set up and well planted needs the minimum of attention, and many are maintained in perfect condition year after year with as little as five minutes a week spent on them. The equipment is inexpensive, and the majority of fishes themselves cost only a few shillings each.

Yet such an Aquarium will provide the beauty of Nature in a small world of its own, measuring perhaps only two cubic feet, a constant living picture that is fascinating and wonderful.

ONE

Setting up an Aquarium

To SET up an aquarium the following items will initially be required:—

		£	s.	d.
The tank (say 24″ × 12″ × 12″) average price		2	10	0
Heater " "			9	6
Thermostat " "			12	6
Strip light & cover glass, or light hood		1	5	0
A sub-sand filter (if desired)			15	0
Thermometer			5	0
Sand and rocks			15	0
Water and plants Plants, say		1	10	0
Total:		£8	2	0

Fish will not be required for a day or two. Then, say,
20 @ 3/- = £3 0 0

Selection of tank

Every beginner should start with a tank as large as can be afforded. Size should be restricted only by price and the amount of room space available. The tank should be rectangular in shape and the height should not greatly exceed the width, for it is the surface area that governs the number of fishes it will hold.

Fishes breathe in oxygen just as we do, and similarly exhale carbon dioxide. Thus, as we extract the oxygen from the air with our lungs, so fish extract dissolved oxygen in the water with their gills. If the water does not contain a good supply of oxygen the fish begin to suffocate and, worse still, they continue to exhale into the water more carbon dioxide all the time. Water can hold only a certain amount of dissolved gases, and unfortunately it can hold more carbon dioxide than it can oxygen, so the situation can easily become critical.

Now, water in any tank is hemmed in at the base and all four sides. The only place the oxygen can enter, and the carbon dioxide disperse, is at the surface. When the surface area is large the interchange is easy and rapid, but when restricted it becomes a bottleneck, and only a little carbon dioxide escapes whilst still less oxygen is able to enter.

As a guide, allow ten sq. inches of surface area to each small fish of about 1″ to 1½″ length. Thus a tank with a surface area of 24″ × 12″ will house roughly twenty-nine small fish.

The larger a tank is the easier it is to keep from fouling quickly. Furthermore, the beginner may wish to increase his stocks of fish as time goes on. The cheapest tanks are those made with an angle-iron framework, with all corners welded at right angles. They have a glass base with four glass sides puttied into the frame. These angle-iron frames are strong and rigid, and may be painted to tone in with the room, the paint also retarding the formation of rust. At a little extra cost the framework can be galvanised, and this prevents rusting for a much longer period.

Where money is not an all-important factor, very nice tanks can be obtained with polished stainless steel framework which is of course rustproof. Also, there are now on the market all-perspex tanks. These are strong, pleasing to look at (being usually bow-fronted), rust-proof, and light to handle when empty.

Position of tank

The position of the tank in the room is important. It should be a focal point and, like a television set, one does not wish to sit with one's head twisted all the time in order to see it. To avoid long trailing leads it should be near an electric plug, which will supply the current for lighting and heating.

Avoid placing the tank in a window, as daylight entering from behind will tend to silhouette the fish and may provide too much light, causing the growth of algae. Also the plants would be likely to turn backwards towards the light, and away from the viewer. Nevertheless, the tank should receive good strong daylight, but not too much sunlight. Therefore a position opposite a window facing north would be almost ideal. It should be placed on an angle-iron stand, or on a stout flat-topped piece of furniture that is about three feet high. It can then be viewed easily and comfortably from a standing or sitting position.

Heating

Tropical fish do not require a great amount of heat. A temperature of 76-78°F. is normal, and this will feel only cool to the hand. This heat is supplied by a heater. Although there are various types on the market, the cheapest and most generally used consist of a 100-120 watt element inside a heat-resisting glass tube, the insulated lead wires passing through a tight rubber cork, then out of the water and by means of a flex connector plug into the thermostat.

Control of heat

Heat is controlled by a thermostat. This can be external or internal, the cheapest and most commonly used being internal. This means that it is suspended in the water on the inside of the tank. Enclosed in a glass tube is a bi-metal strip which expands and contracts on heating and cooling. One of the strips of metal expands more than the other. Being welded together this causes the bi-metal strip to curve slightly, thus producing a make-and-break in the electric circuit. To prevent interference with radio or television a small magnet is incorporated, to provide a snap action both on and off. An external knob permits the thermostat to be adjusted.

Once set to come on at 76°F. it should remain in contact; thus the current passes through it and thence to the heater, and slowly warms up the water until it reaches 78°F. The extra warmth accordingly expands the bi-metal strip, which eventually curves, and finally snaps open, thus cutting the current and leaving the heater to cool down. Naturally, the water begins to cool slightly, and when it drops below 76° the bi-metal strip in the thermostat contracts, straightens, and snaps shut once more. The whole cycle may take a couple of hours according to the room temperature, but the current would have been on only part of this time, so consumption is very small.

Lighting

The aquarium will need to be lighted so that the fishes can be seen, and most tanks are sold with an over-all light hood covering the entire top of the tank; or, if preferred, a strip light can be used. When a strip light is employed the remainder of the un-covered part of the top of the tank will need to be covered by strong glass, because tropical fishes do quite frequently jump out of the water.

To set up a tank

Having purchased the tank, heater, thermostat, light hood etc., and chosen the site where it will stand, the next thing to do is to test the tank for leaks. It should be stood on a flat concrete or linoleum-covered floor and filled with water. If there is a very small leak the water pressure, dirt and dust seeping through may block it; but if the leak is worse, take the tank back to the shop and have it exchanged for another.

Once satisfied that it is water-tight, empty it, and set it on its stand. If a sub-gravel filter is to be used (*see* p. 33) this must be installed now.

Sand

Sand is now required, and any old sand will not do. If it is too fine the roots of the plants will not be able to penetrate; if too coarse, particles of food will fall between the grains out of reach of the fish, and will rot. One-sixteenth grade sand is recommended. It should be thoroughly washed in an enamel bucket many times, until the water poured off is quite clear. Only then is it fit for use in the aquarium. Spread it evenly over the bottom, (covering the sub-sand filter, if used) so that there is a depth of 1″ in front, and roughly 1¼″ at the back.

Rockwork

Rocks will make the aquarium look more natural, and should preferably be of natural water-worn stone. Chippings approxi-mately 5″ or 6″ across can usually be bought from plant nurseries which sell large blocks of stone for use on rockeries. Avoid crystal or glass. These materials have too sharp edges on which the fish can damage themselves. Chalk and limestone rocks may slowly dissolve in the water, making it hard and alkaline by the addition of lime.

Rocks should not be put in haphazardly. To place a large piece

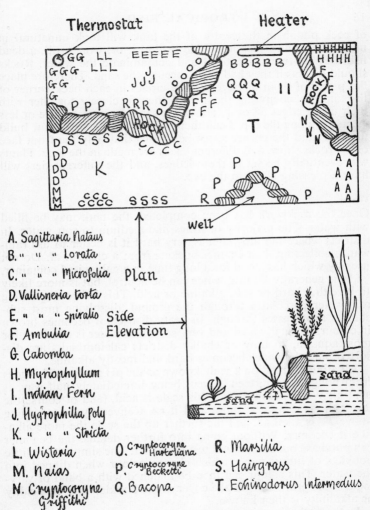

A. Sagittaria Nataus
B. " " " Lorata
C. " " " Microfolia
D. Vallisneria torta
E. " " " spiralis
F. Ambulia
G. Cabomba
H. Myriophyllum
I. Indian Fern
J. Hygrophilla Poly
K. " " " Stricta
L. Wisteria
M. Naias
N. Cryptocoryne Griffithi
O. Cryptocoryne Hartoliana
P. Cryptocoryne Beckeiti
Q. Bacopa
R. Marsilia
S. Hairgrass
T. Echinodorus Intermedius

Plan

Side Elevation

Well

Fig. 1. Diagram showing a typical aquarium-planting scheme, with the sand tiered by use of rock work.

15

of rock plumb in the centre of the tank will look unnatural in most cases, and fishes may hide behind it or, worse still, a dead fish may lie there unnoticed and contaminate the water. Rocks should look as if they had worn through the sand. Therefore place flat pieces of them on edge in semi-circles in each back corner of the tank, manoeuvring them until they fit closely together with their upper edges 3″ or 4″ above the sand, making a more or less even line along the top. Lean them slightly backwards. Now build up with sand the corner space behind so that only the front face of the rocks show, and different levels are made in the tank. Plants will eventually be set in these ledges, and the different tiers will have a pleasing effect to the eye.

Water

Once the rockwork has been completed, the tank may be filled with water. The majority of fishes like medium to soft water. In districts where the tap-water is very hard it is better to use rain-water, collecting it in enamel buckets from a clean roof. Do not use any which has stood for a long time in a galvanised container.

As is generally known, water can be neutral, but is more likely to be either hard or soft, alkaline or acid. This is because falling rain-water percolates through the ground, dissolving most substances as it passes through. In peaty districts it becomes brown in colour, is usually acid and very soft. This water is excellent for most aquaria. In limy or chalky districts calcium salts are dissolved, and the water becomes hard and mostly alkaline.

Alkalinity is read on a scale known as the pH reading. This goes from nought to fourteen. Seven, being immediately half-way, is neutral. Water below 7·0 on this scale is acid, (and of course the lower the reading, the more acid it is). Conversely, water rating above 7·0 is alkaline, and the further up the scale the more alkaline it becomes. Without going into further details, the beginner can purchase outfits that will test the water. The simplest are little booklets of litmus paper which change colour when dipped into the water. This colour can then be matched with a band of varying colours printed inside the cover of the booklet, and the acidity or alkalinity is then known.

In the author's opinion a great deal of fuss is made over pH, but after thirty years' experience in breeding tropical fish he finds that pH makes little difference. In any case altering the pH will not ensure a standard reading. Unless the solution is buffered the water will soon revert to its original reading. Even carbon dioxide in the air will alter the pH slightly – and this occurs every day and every night.

On the other hand hardness, which has for so long been ignored, is in the author's opinion of great importance. An outfit may be bought for about three guineas, (the test being known as titrating) which will give an accurate reading of the hardness of the water in parts per millon of calcium carbonate as well as magnesium salts. This need not trouble the beginner, but advanced breeders wishing to reproduce fishes such as neon tetras and cardinals cannot be consistently successful unless they ensure that the water in the breeding tank is extremely soft. Certainly one might by sheer luck obtain the right amount of hardness, but it will be impossible to do this continually without taking steps to soften the water to the correct figure.

Water softeners are expensive pieces of equipment, and are not recommended for softening water that is to be used for breeding fishes.

Filling the tank

When filling the tank, in order not to disturb the rockwork which has already been placed in position, put a saucer in the front of the tank and on it stand a jam-jar. Gently warm up the rain-water in an enamel pail on a gas-ring to 78°F., and with an enamel jug pour it slowly into the jam-jar. Allow it to trickle over on to the saucer, and thence on to the sand. This will break its fall, and if done carefully no sand will be disturbed. Once the saucer is completely under water, pouring can be done more rapidly.

Fill the tank only about seven-eighths full. This allows one to insert the forearm when setting the plant roots in the sand.

Thermometer

The thermometer should be placed in the tank for a few minutes and read. Here one has the choice of two types. There is the long tubular type, containing either mercury or spirit. Mercury is a little more expensive, but often more accurate. When buying a thermometer hold several in the hand, and choose one of any that read the same.

These thermometers may be of the floating type, or ones that

can be attached by a rubber circular disc to the front glass of the
aquarium. The floating ones are, on the whole, more useful.

There is another type of thermometer in the form of a dial. It
is constructed with a rubber flange which sticks to the front glass
of the tank. A needle moves round the dial and comes to rest at
the temperature of the water. These instruments are very good,
and are not too conspicuous.

TWO

Plants

THE AQUARIUM will require plants. They make an attractive picture, offer shade and refuge for the fishes, and play an important part in keeping the tank clear and clean.

Most of the aquaria seen are under-planted. These are not so pleasing in appearance, and more time has to be spent on maintenance. It will be well worth while to spend as much money as possible on plants. The following varieties are suggested as being the easiest and cheapest for beginners to obtain.

SAGITTARIA. There are three or four species. *S. natans* is a grassy plant with leaves about 8-10″ long and ¼″ wide. It forms a good background in the deep parts of the tank. *S. lorata* is similar, but not so tall, and can be used in the middle distance. *S. microfolia* is a pretty little plant with tiny swordlike leaves, but grows to a height of only 2″. It makes an excellent carpet in the foreground. All these plants reproduce by sending out runners.

VALLISNERIA. This is another grassy plant, but the leaves are thinner, broader and more tapelike. *V. spiralis* grows to about 12-14″ in height and can be used as an alternative, or additional, background. *V. torta* has corkscrew-shaped leaves that grow to a height of 10″. It is most attractive, but not so hardy as the *Sagittarias* and generally prefers a stronger light. Reproduction is by runners.

LIMNOPHILA SESSILIFLORA, (Ambulia). This is a pale green plant with feathery fronds that sprout from a central stem like the spokes of a wheel, forming small circles. It has an attractive rosette head. It likes plenty of light, and grows to an average height of 10″. When the stems grow too tall they should be nipped off, half-way down, and the cutting planted.

CABOMBA. There are several species, all much alike. From a central stem pairs of leaves on a small stalk branch outwards like the ribs of a fan. It is less compact than ambulia, a slightly darker green, and sometimes becomes too straggly; but when in a situation to its liking it is a strong grower, and bears enormous heads, rosette in shape. Reproduction by cuttings.

MYRIOPHYLLUM. Again three or four species, the commonest being *M. verticillatum*. Small feathery leaves branch out from the whole length of the stem. Each leaf similarly bears small stems upon it, giving the plant a very feathery appearance. It requires strong light, and must be kept free of thread algae, which will entangle and smother it. Reproduction by cuttings.

CERATOPTERIS, (Indian fern). There are two species, the broad and the fine. Both are typical ferns. Under strong light they grow rapidly, and produce young plants from the edges of their leaves in such profusion that they are apt to make the plant buoyant, and it may arise out of the sand when too big. The young plants, if knocked off the parent, will float to the surface. Once they have attained long enough roots they may be planted in the sand and soon replace the parent, which has now become straggly and old.

HYGROPHILA. Two species. *H. polysperma* bears bright green, lanceolate leaves from a central stem. It requires plenty of light, and can be reproduced by cuttings or layers. *H. stricta* is a much larger plant, and makes an excellent centrepiece as each leaf can be 6″ long × 1½″ wide. When too tall the head should be pinched out and replanted. The base will then throw several forks. A single leaf with the stem planted in the sand will soon take root and form a new plant. Its only drawback appears to be that snails appreciate its taste, and will bore holes in the leaves.

SYNEMMA TRIFLORUM, (water wisteria). An excellent plant, with pale green broken-edged leaves, somewhat similar in general appearance to Indian ferns, except that the leaves here grow from a central stem. Reproduction by layering or cuttings. An easy grower: a single leaf planted in the sand will root and form a new plant. Excellent for the middle of the aquarium.

NAIAS MICRODON. This is a very brittle, but quick-growing plant. It has spear-shaped leaves growing from a central stem. The lower ends of the stems may be pushed into the sand where they will root easily; but it will grow just as well when left floating below the surface of the water. Requires a strong light. Stems bunched together make a colourful feathery clump.

CRYPTOCORYNES, excellent long-lived plants, that do well in subdued light. There are numerous species, all of them slightly different. *C. ciliata* is large and will make a fine centrepiece, but is not too easy to grow. Neither is it usually cheap. *C. griffithi* bears large leaves on long stiff stems reaching a height of 12″; it occasionally flowers under water. Not always obtainable. *C. harteliana*, probably the best choice for the beginner. The long lanceolate leaves are dark green on the top, and reddish-purple below. Unlike others of the genus, it grows rapidly by runners. These it sends out in great profusion, soon making a tremendous thicket. Size about 10″, does not require too much light. Though there are several other good species, one that deserves mention is *C. beckettii*. This is one of the miniatures, and excellent in the fore part of the aquarium. The leaves are bright green on both sides, but the stems tend to spread outwards. Occasionally sends out a runner, but is best dug up once a year and divided.

BACOPA CAROLINIANA. Small oval leaves grow from a stiff central stem, which reaches a height of 8-12″. This plant is a bright green, and its erect method of growth makes a welcome change. Reproduction by cuttings.

MARSILEA QUADRIFOLIA, (four-leafed clover). A pretty little plant which grows from runners in a straight line. Each stem bears four clover-like leaves at its tip. Under too strong a light the stems grow far too tall, and the leaves reach the water surface where they are hardly seen, only stems being visible. In subdued light it remains short and compact, and is ideal for a front corner of the tank.

ELEOCHARIS ACICULARIS, (Hair grass). As the name implies, these are needle-like leaves which grow in a bunch. Its light appearance gives a dainty effect, and it is ideal in front of rocks as it usually reaches a height of only 5″. Reproduction by runners.

FLOATING PLANTS

There are various floating plants. They have their uses, but in a community tank they are likely to spread over the surface of the water and prevent the electric light above from reaching the plants rooted in the sand below. Their roots hang down below the water surface, and in a community tank are not always decorative. Thus, unless required for a special purpose, they are not advisable in this sort of tank.

Although there are many more tropical plants most of these are not so easily obtained, and are somewhat expensive. All have their distinct beauty, and to those beyond the beginner's stage are heartily recommended such plants as *Aponogeton*, *A. ulvaceus*, *A. undulatum*, as well as the fabulous Madagascar lace leaf plant – *A. fenestralis*. Another large and beautiful plant is the Amazon sword plant, *Echinodorus intermedius*, and its cousin *E. radicans*, both bearing beautiful large leaves.

Fig. 1 on page 15 suggests how some of these plants can be placed in the aquarium.

It will be noted that the tallest plants are put in the deepest parts of the tank, with the shorter plans in the foreground and in the back corner tiers. These back corners often receive the least amount of light, so are reserved for those plants which can do with a little less light. However, the position of the tank makes a big difference. If more light is entering from a window on the left hand side it may be necessary to place some of the feathery plants closer to this source of illumination.

Tropical aquatic plants are quite easy to grow, and one does not have to be a skilled gardener to reproduce them. Most reproduce by cuttings, runners or layers, and some by detaching young plants growing from the leaves of the parent. A few can be grown from seed, but this is no job for the beginner. Growth is dependent on two things: light and nourishment. In fact, the clarity and cleanliness of any aquarium is dependent mainly on the plants, as we shall see.

Under strong light plants absorb carbon dioxide which they break down into sugars and starches for food. As this process, called photo synthesis, is taking place oxygen is released into the water. Thus lack of light will starve the plants, and they will lose their fresh green colour, turn brown and wither away. Too much light, on the other hand, will tend to force them, making them long and spindly, and a pale yellowy-green.

Most beginners wonder how much light they should use. One cannot lay down a regular scale. Each tank differs according to its situation. The main thing is to see that new shoots or new green tips are sprouting regularly on the plants. This shows that they are receiving enough light, that photo synthesis is taking place, and that they are growing. But if at the same time green algae begins to grow on the rocks, the plant leaves, and the walls of the aquarium, then a little too much light is being given. Plants can only absorb as much light as they require. Any excess cannot be used up by them, so Nature tries to burn up this extra light by growing more plants in the form of tiny cells called algae, which may take several forms.

These may be in such abundance that they turn the water green in colour; or the cells may link and grow as minute hairs on the leaves of the plants, or form threadlike strands among the stems of plants. Often in extremely strong light there is a dark, almost black, leathery green skin which in its early stages can be peeled off like adhesive tape. There are two alternative cures – one or the other is the only answer. Either (i) cut down the light a little, say by one hour a day, until the aquarium plants absorb all that is going and there is no excess left to feed the algae, or (ii) put more plants into the aquarium so that they use up the light entering, and once again there is no excess to feed the algae.

Plants also play another part. They all have roots, whether floating from the surface or anchored in the sand. As old leaves die off these, as well as fish droppings, form a sediment which sinks on to the sand. Here it is converted by bacteria into nitrogenous material which the hungry plant roots absorb to rebuild new tissue and leaves. Without this nutriment they will be weak and unable to thrive. When there are few plants in the aquarium but a good number of fish, the deposit of mulm will build up on the surface of the sand, and many aquarists complain that they are forced to siphon this off at least once a week to keep the aquarium moderately clean. This is not reaching the basis of the trouble. The reason is too many fish and too few plants. Reverse this, so that there are fewer fishes and plenty of plants, and the small amount of sediment (mulm) formed will be drawn down through the sand and feasted upon by the plant roots.

A well-planted aquarium rarely needs any siphoning. It must be repeated that plenty of plants will prevent the growth of algae. This means that the tank does not have to be scraped to clean the glass, and plenty of plants will absorb the mulm, which in turn means that siphoning away the excess will not become necessary.

THREE

Planting

P LANTS PURCHASED at a shop, or obtained from a nursery
by post, should arrive damp, labelled, and rolled up in plastic
sheeting.

Before setting them in a tank rinse them under a running tap,
and place them in a basin of water. Keep the various species
apart. The taller plants with roots, such as Vallisneria, Sagittaria,
or Cryptocorynes should be planted towards the back of the
aquarium; Vallisneria and Sagittaria in the deeper parts, and the
Cryptocorynes in the back corner tiers.

With the thumb and third finger hold the root of each plant,
and then with the first finger wiggle rather than push the roots
under the sand. The roots will then be horizontal in the sand,
and the crown of the plant should just show at sand level. Place
those of the same species near each other, say 1″ apart, so that a
line or thicket of one type is formed.

Continue planting with the medium height plants, working
across the tank, and coming slowly towards the front as progress
is made.

Cuttings without roots, such as stems of Ambulia, Cabomba or
Myriophyllum, should be bunched together at the foot of the
stem, four or five stems to each bunch. Treat the lower $1\frac{1}{2}″$ of
these stems exactly as roots, pushing them horizontally under the
sand as before.

Finally, set the shorter, smaller plants such as *S. microfolia,*
four-leafed clover, *C. beckettii* etc. in the front or foreground of
the tank. When all is done add a little more water so that the level
of the surface is hidden by the lower edge of the top angle of the
tank. To leave a tank even $\frac{1}{4}″$ below this one sees the surface of
the water, and this is unattractive. When the surface is out of
view the tank appears as if there were no water in it at all.

Now leave them severely alone in order that the newly-set

plants may strike and get a hold to start growing without further disturbance.

Give them about six to eight hours of electric light a day to encourage quick rooting – and watch the thermometer. If the water remains between 76-78°F. all is well. If not, adjust the thermostat slightly to increase or decrease the warmth of the water, as required. Make small adjustments each time so that the desired temperature is gradually achieved. Thermostats should function accurately within two or three degrees, so turning the control knob even a quarter turn may make a very great difference.

By now the water in the tank may look a little cloudy. Planting slightly disturbs the sand, and tiny particles of dust soon rise from it, in spite of the thorough washing it has already gone through. However, it does not take long for these microscopic particles to become waterlogged and sink; and within three days the water should be so clear that it is hard to believe that there is any in the aquarium at all.

Take a good look, and remember that this is how the tank should always remain in future – sweet, clean, and sparklingly clear. If it does not, there are three causes – (i) too much light causing the growth of algae, (ii) too little light, so that the plants are dying back and not performing their proper function, or (iii) overfeeding the fish; too much food sinking uneaten into the sand, where it rots, becoming a breeding-ground for bacteria which will soon become a thick culture and, seen in their millions, the water will be a cloudy grey and evil-smelling.

Assuming that all is clear, and new green tips or runners on the plants are noticeable, that the temperature is steady, etc., fish can now be introduced.

The aquarist must decide at this stage whether he wishes to keep just one species of fish, or to go in for a varied collection – known as a community tank. With the former a delightful shoal of fish, generally keeping together, is very pleasing; with the latter one has variety, but the species will disport themselves more or less separately throughout the tank.

In either case smaller fish are recommended at first. It is a mistake to buy too many at once. Starting in a small way the cost will be less, and should there be a disaster the loss can be borne more easily, and a new start made later; whereas a big loss may be so heavy and irreplaceable that the earlier work and expenditure are totally wasted. In any case, having gained a little experience it is both interesting and exciting to add more fish from time to time.

Choose species that will get along well together. Bullies can do a lot of damage and cause considerable trouble.

Avoid fish that have a tendency to nibble the plants. It is heartbreaking to have an aquarium containing beautiful plants reduced in a few days to one or two leafless stumps. As fast as the plants try to grow they are chopped back; without leaves they cannot breathe or obtain the sugar and starches they require. Very soon they will be useless; and since they cannot perform their proper function it will be only a short while before the water in the aquarium becomes cloudy.

Any of the following species may be selected as safe and suitable for the beginner:—

LIVE-BEARERS

Glarydichthys falcates (Blue eyes)
Lebistes reticulatus (Guppies)
Mollienisia latipinna (Mollies)

Phallichthys amates (Merry Widows)
Platypoecillus maculatus (Platys)

EGG-LAYERS

Acanthophthalmus semicinctus (Kuhli eels)
Ambassis lala. (Glass fish)
Aphyocharax rubipinnis (Bloodfin)
Barbus gelius (Miniature barbs)
Barbus nigrofasciatus (Ruby barbs)
Barbus oligolepis (Chequer barb)
Barbus titteya (Cherry barb)
Brachydania albolineatus (Pearl danio)
Brachydonio nigrofasciatus (Spotted danio)
Brachydanio rerio (Zebra danio)
Cheirodon axelrodi (Cardinal tetra)
Colisa lalia (Dwarf gourami)
Corydoras aeneus (Bronze catfish)
Corydoras julii (Leopard catfish)
Corydoras paleatus (Mottled catfish)
Epiplatys chaperi (Orange-throated panchax)

Gyrinocheilus aymonieri (Sucking loach)
Hyphessobrychon callistus minor (Minor tetra)
Hyphessobrycon serpae (Serpae tetra)
Hyphessobrycon innesi (Neon tetra)
Hyphessobrycon pulchripinnis (Lemon tetra)
Hyphessobrycon roseaceus (Rosy tetra)
Nannostomus anomalus (Pencil fish)
Otocinclus affinis (Sucking catfish)
Pristella riddlei (X-ray fish)
Pterophyllum eimekei (Angel fish)
Rasbora heteromorpha (Harlequin)
Rasbora pauciperforata (Glowlight rasbora)
Tanichthys albonubes (White Cloud Mountain Minnow)
Thayeria sanctemaria (Penguin)

With any selection is recommended at least one Kuhli eel or a
Catfish as these species act as scavengers, seeking out particles of
foodstuffs that sink on to the sand, which might otherwise rot.

Further details of these and other fishes start on p. 62.

Fishes purchased will either be in jars, or more likely in polythene bags. If they have come a long way by passenger train the
bag will contain water, and be blown up with oxygen and securely
tied. The bag will then have been placed in a cardboard box lined
with straw or crumpled newspaper. All this ensures that the fishes
will have plenty of oxygen during their journey, and the insulation will prevent too much heat loss.

On receiving the fishes the ideal is to quarantine them for a
period of ten days in a separate unplanted tank at a temperature
of 78-80°F. Should disease break out on the fishes they can be
treated in the empty tank, and since there are no plants any treatment given will have no harmful effects on the plant life. However,
most beginners will not have a spare tank and must take the risk
of putting the newly bought fishes into the aquarium.

Do not tip the fish straight into the tank. If they are in jars
place a hand over the top and pour surplus water down the sink,
leaving the jar half-full. This jar is then floated in the aquarium,
and the cover glass put over it. If the fishes are in a plastic bag
do not open it. Place the whole bag, still sealed, into the tank,
where it will float. Leave for twenty minutes. This again will
ensure that the water temperature of the newly-acquired fish and
that in the tank will equalise, and there will be no shock when the
fish are finally turned out.

As explained earlier, waters differ, and it may be that the water
in the jars or bag is slightly different from that in the aquarium.
When the fishes are being released endeavour to allow a little of
the aquarium water to flow into the bag or jars. Tip a little in
and out for a few minutes so that the waters become mixed and
equalise, and once again there is no shock to the fishes' system.

Make sure of course that no fish is left stranded in either a jam
jar or bag, and that all have swum happily into the aquarium.

Tank Maintenance

As stated earlier, an aquarium that is not overcrowded with fishes
and which is well and thickly planted, given the correct amount

of light, kept at the normal temperature, and not overfed, requires very little cleaning, if at all. The author has tanks which have maintained themselves in perfect condition for over ten years, without any cleaning of any kind. The water is absolutely clear, there is no algae, no excess mulm. The only attention they have received during this time is the thinning out of the plants about once a year, and topping up the small amount of water that evaporates.

In large Tropical Fish hatcheries there is too much to do with breeding thousands of fish, feeding, sorting, catching, selling and transportation, to spend money and time on cleaning operations. If these establishments can maintain hundreds of tanks with little or no cleaning, then an aquarist with one tank should be able to do the same. However, should this ideal not be carried out there are on the market various pieces of equipment that can aid the cleaning of aquaria.

Equipment

For removing algae from the glass walls of the tank there is a long handled scraper into which can be fixed old razor blades. The point of operation is set at an angle, and when moved up and down the algae is easily scraped away. After a few minutes the algae settles on the sand and it can be removed, together with any excess mulm, by a siphon tube.

This needs to be of $\frac{1}{4}''$ diameter rubber tubing, and should be long enough to reach from inside the bottom of the tank, over the top, down to the floor, and up again about three feet. Place one end in the tank about half-way down, and suck the other end of the tube. Water will enter the tube, but long before it has reached the aquarist's mouth the tube is pinched, and the end taken out of the mouth and placed in an enamel bucket standing on the floor. As soon as one ceases to pinch the tube, water will flow into the bucket, and when the end of the tube in the tank is lowered near the sand and moved gently about, the mulm will be sucked up and deposited in the bucket. Again, if left for a few minutes the mulm will settle in the bottom of the bucket, and the clear water can be carefully poured into an enamel jug and put back in the tank. If any sand has been siphoned out as well this remains in the bottom of the bucket, but after one or two washes under a tap is quickly cleaned, and can also be returned to the aquarium.

Generally speaking, the simplest equipment is best, and it is not necessary for the beginner to go out and buy all sorts of articles. Wait until these are found to be absolutely necessary. Nevertheless, listed below are some articles which may be found of use.

1. Jam-jars. A good supply of 2 lb jam-jars is invaluable. They are excellent for equalising temperatures when introducing fishes into a tank; for examining an off-colour specimen; for treating a single fish when attacked by a disease; and for transporting fishes to Shows etc.

2. Nets. These may be bought at most Pet Stores. The majority today are made from nylon mesh as this material lasts a very long time, although continually soaked and dried, day in and day out. There are a few nets which are difficult to obtain in shops, but these can be made quite simply at home. Always make sure that the bowl, or depth, of the net is at least one and a half times its width, so that when a fish is caught one can enclose it with the fingers in a sort of bag, making sure that it will not jump out and land on the floor.

Fine nylon of the type used for making shirts and blouses made into a net and attached to a very strong frame, will be found excellent as a strainer. Dirty water from the aquarium when poured through this net will be almost crystal clear in the bucket below.

A tiny net of about 1½″ diameter is also useful for getting a fish out of a jam-jar, and for sorting sizes of young fry.

It is as well to have a spare heater and possibly a thermostat, the former being more important, as should the one in the tank break the spare may be fitted. This sort of accident usually occurs at night or during a week-end, when one cannot just go around the corner and buy another.

Feeding rings

These are usually made of plastic tubing in the form of a ring or square. They float on the water surface, and dried food sprinkled inside the ring is prevented from spreading all over the water surface. Any that sinks will be beneath the ring, and is more easily siphoned off, should too much be given. The disadvantage of rings is that they confine the food to a small area and the larger fishes get the lion's share. When food is spread all over the surface the smaller fishes cannot so easily be driven away from it.

Worm basket

These are excellent and are much like the feeding ring, except that there is a perforated bowl of plastic beneath the upper rim. This floats just below the surface of the water, and small worms placed in the basket slowly wriggle through the holes more or less one by one, so that the fishes can eat them before they reach the bottom and burrow into the sand.

Channel rubber

A few feet of channel rubber can be cut the height of the tank and with a sheet of glass will form an almost watertight compartment. Thus a tank can be divided if necessary into one, two or three divisions.

Planting sticks

These are usually straight pieces of metal with a notch at the bottom. They enable one to put in an extra plant amongst the others already growing, difficult to do by hand; but unless these are used very carefully there is every likelihood that the sharp point will shear the roots of the plant completely away.

Traps

For those intending to breed fishes traps are sometimes useful. These are usually made of plastic or stainless steel mesh. They allow the eggs or, in the case of live-bearers, baby fishes to drop through the interstices to safety, whilst the parents are unable to follow and devour them. Of course in a community tank there needs to be a second compartment to the trap which is below and boxed in, so that the eggs or fry cannot be swallowed by the other fishes swimming freely in the tank.

Pumps

In time perhaps the aquarist may wish to have a pump, and this should be purchased at a Pet Stores. They are operated either by a diaphragm or by small pistons, and force air down a tube to the bottom of the aquarium. In order to make the bubbles as fine as possible at the end of the tube there is a diffuser stone, rather like pumice stone, so that the air does not come out in large bubbles, but as a very fine spray. Pumps will also operate filters, but instead of a diffuser stone a plastic tube, called an air lift, is used.

This plastic tube reaches to the bottom of the tank, but the aerator tube enters it about an inch or two above its lowest point. Usually the other end is curved over, so that air and water coming out will be spilled in a certain direction. When the tube is inserted in the tank, water enters it, and when the pump is switched on bubbles rise up the tube. As each is surrounded by water, both air and water are lifted and ejected from the spout. The spout may be placed inside an internal filter.

This is a plastic basket, perforated along its base, held inside the tank by clips, into which is put a bottom layer of small pebbles, a middle layer of activated carbon, and a top layer of silver sand or cotton wool. Water from the air lift spilled into the basket trickles through the layers and back into the tank. The cotton wool traps small particles of sediment. The activated carbon will absorb unwanted gases, and the small pebbles merely allow the water to flow back without restriction.

The cotton wool can be replaced every so often, and once every year the activated carbon should be taken out and baked in an oven for a short while so that the gases are driven out. It is then ready for re-use.

Outside filters are much the same but generally larger, and therefore capable of doing much more work. This filter usually takes the form of a large battery jar in a frame, or maybe sheets of glass glazed in a frame, similar to a tank. The frame has two hooks on it to hang on the top rim of the aquarium. The filter is divided into two sections by a sheet of glass which has a small notch cut out of the bottom of it. One compartment is usually much larger than the other. The large compartment contains the filter medium in its three layers. The clear compartment has an air lift in it with the spout protruding over the top of the frame. A separate piece of plastic tubing bent over at one end like a walking-stick is dipped into the tank and allowed to fill with water. The handle end is then covered with a finger, and lifted so that the spout enters the large compartment of the filter; and because the top level of the sand or cotton wool in the filter is lower than the water in the tank, the walking-stick tube acts as a

Photo: Pace

1. *Mollienisia latipinna* (Green Molly)

2. *Thayeria sancte-maria* (Penguin fish)

3. *Pterophyllum eimekei*
Black Lace Angel (right)
Common Angel (left)

4. *Barbus gelius*
(Miniature barb)

5. *Otocinclus affinis*
(Sucking Catfish)

Photo: Pace

6. *Rasbora hetero-
morpha* (Harlequin)

Photo: Kathleen Cooke

7. *Barbus nigrofascia-
tus* (Ruby barb)

Photo: Kathleen Cooke

siphon and water pours into the filter medium. Having gone through all the three layers it is now clear and pours through the notch in the dividing glass, filling the smaller empty compartment. When the pump is attached to the air lift water is lifted and runs back into the aquarium. As the water level in the filter compartment drops, more siphons in through the walking-stick tube. Thus the circulation continues until the pump is stopped.

Where a sub-sand filter is used the principle is not quite the same. The air lift sends air and water up a plastic stem, and tips it back into the aquarium at the surface of the water; but as air and water rise up the stem more clear water takes their place in the tubes beneath the sand, so that a circulation is set up. But now the sand is acting as the filter medium, catching between its grains the particles of mulm, and only clear water flows into the tubes beneath the sand.

However, as stated before, plants require some mulm from which their roots obtain nourishment. Thus in a continually filtered tank the plants are apt to be undernourished and not do so well.

It must be emphasised that if an aquarium is properly set up with plenty of plants and not overcrowded with fish, no filters are necessary. Fishes exist in the wild in ponds and river tributaries. These are not equipped with aerators or filters. Had they been necessary Nature would have seen to it that they were provided. These filters are not natural, and one cannot do better than imitate Nature, so really one should be able to keep an aquarium clear and healthy without such artificial aids.

It must also be borne in mind that a pump will circulate the water which, when it reaches the surface, is able to discharge the carbon dioxide and replenish with oxygen. When it is circulating in this way the water is able to hold its maximum amount of oxygen, and the fish capacity of a tank can be doubled. But this is a dangerous practice, for when the pump is not operating the tank is definitely overcrowded, and should it cease because of an electric power cut or from a mechanical breakdown (particularly if this happens whilst the aquarist is away for several hours), he may come home to find many of his fish dead from suffocation, and others hanging just below the water surface gasping for oxygen. With a tank that has the right number of fishes, or is slightly understocked, such a disaster cannot happen.

B

FOUR

Foods

Dried foods

There are on the market many different manufactured dried foods. Some are good, others are poor. A dried food should contain all the essential ingredients of a balanced diet. These are proteins, fats, carbohydrates, vegetable matter, mineral salts and vitamins. These should be in correct proportions and the food should be finely ground, so that even quite small fishes can take and digest it.

These manufactured dried foods are easy to use, and will keep for a reasonable period. Consequently they are a good stand-by as the basis of the fishes' diet. Most are highly concentrated and must be used very sparingly. Feed only as much as the fishes will eat up in ten minutes. Probably fewer fishes die of starvation than are killed by overfeeding, obesity and pollution.

If the portions are over-large much of the food will sink rapidly to the bottom, falling between the grains of sand, out of the fishes' reach and quickly turn rotten, thus soon fouling the water. The better dried foods float for a long period and do not foul so easily.

Remember, no matter how good a dried food may be, fishes enjoy a change of diet occasionally.

Fresh and frozen foods

About once or twice a week, when these are used, the regular meal of dried food should not be given. Few aquarists realise how many varied suitable foods they have available, quite often in their larder. The following make excellent fish foods:– cold cooked meat or fish, liver, heart etc. A small knob chopped finely with a razor blade will be taken eagerly. Also fresh or frozen prawn, shrimp, crab etc. Use only about one-quarter of a shrimp at a time.

34

Very, very occasionally a tiny knob of grated cheddar cheese will make a meal, and a minute portion of the yolk of a hard-boiled egg pushed through a tea-strainer can be served. If there is no algae in the tank, the tiniest amount of tinned spinach will be enjoyed.

Cultured foods

These are those which can be bred, and thus there is always a small supply of living food on hand. For very small fry, micro-worm is a good food. A culture of these minute worms can be purchased at many Pet Shops. Prepare a small saucerful of ground oatmeal, or some prepared baby food, mixed with a small amount of water. Place the culture of worms in the centre of this, cover with a glass, and shade with a piece of cardboard. The worms will multiply so rapidly that they become overcrowded. They climb the sides of the saucer in an effort to escape. There they can be wiped off with a finger and fed to fry and other small fishes. The culture will remain active for about ten days; so before it becomes too foul start a second saucer, and even a third, at intervals of five days, each being started off from the previous culture. The trio of saucers can be used in rotation. Keep at a temperature of 70-75°F.

For slightly larger fishes one may culture grindal worms. These are best bred in shallow wooden boxes containing a mixture of fine soil, peat or leaf mould, which must be kept damp. On it place the culture, brought from a Pet Shop, and feed with porridge or baby cereal mixed with milk. Feed only sufficient, so that the worms clear it up each day. Over the box place a sheet of glass, and again cover with cardboard to exclude the light. Within a few days the worms will have multiplied, and when the cover glass is lifted many will be adhering to the underside. These should be scraped off with a razor blade and fed direct into the tank, or into the worm basket previously described. These worms prefer to be kept at a temperature of about 70-75°F.

Enchytrae

Commonly known as white worms. These are larger than grindal worms, and are cultured in exactly the same way, except that they prefer a temperature of 60-65°F.

Earth worms

If one has a garden, and potato skins, dead leaves etc. are piled in one spot, small pink garden worms will soon frequent the heap, provided it is kept shady and damp. A few can be collected at a time. They should be chopped with a razor blade into small portions, washed in a net under a running tap, and the clean particles fed to the fish. This is an unpleasant job, but the fish really enjoy such an occasional feed.

Live pond foods

During the spring and summer months daphnia, a small crustacean, may be collected in ponds. One needs a large shallow net with a long handle, and by gently moving this backwards and forwards through the water daphnia, if present, may be collected. A little, say not more than a cupful, should be tipped into a can of water and taken home. They should then be put into a clean enamel basin and examined. Daphnia look something like fleas. In fact they are often called water fleas. They are harmless and cannot bite, and do not usually survive long in captivity, even in clean water, and of course die very quickly when taken out of water. They have a curious hopping motion when swimming, and fishes attracted by the movement, quickly gorge themselves.

Be careful not to introduce any other creature that looks dangerous. These are more easily seen if daphnia is first tipped into an enamel basin before being placed in the aquarium. Most of the goodness in daphnia is in the juicy interior, the outer shell being little more than roughage. Thus fish fed on daphnia look plump immediately after it, but the food value is not very lasting.

Cyclops are smaller than daphnia, and look rather like an old-fashioned bomb complete with fins. Actually these are egg-sacs on the female. Males do not have these bomb fins. Fishes will eat cyclops readily, but find them more difficult to catch as they are quicker than daphnia, and of course being smaller more are required for food. Cyclops should not be fed into breeding tanks as they will catch and devour the newly hatched fry of egg-laying fishes.

In winter one should be able to catch, with the same type of net, glass worms in the ponds. These are almost transparent, about $\frac{1}{3}''$ long, and have a hook over their mouths. They make a good food for medium-sized fishes, but are dangerous with fry.

Occasionally one finds in water-butts and old baths kept in the open, mosquito and gnat larvae which come up to the surface to breathe. A quick scoop with the net will often capture many of them, and they make an excellent food. More can be placed in the aquarium at one time than any of the above-mentioned pond foods, as they breathe atmospheric air, and will not deplete the tank of oxygen. Daphnia, cyclops, and glass worms, will extract oxygen from the water, so too many should not be put in the tank at one time.

Blood worms are excellent food, but are difficult to obtain. Occasionally one finds them in old water-butts. They are about $\frac{1}{2}''$ long and a very bright red. They have more food value than any of the foregoing.

Tubifex

These are long thin worms usually found in rivers and ponds where sewage is discharged. It is a filthy job collecting them, the mud and tubifex being placed in an old stocking or other form of fine strainer. The stocking is then placed in a bucket of water and the worms wriggle free. They are reddish-brown in colour. They live in filth, and may bring with them all sorts of unwanted bacteria. Though commonly used, the author does not recommend them. Experience shows that fishes continually fed with tubifex worms sicken, or may develop boils and other troubles. As there are so many good foods that are harmless it would seem unnecessary to take any risk with tubifex.

FIVE

Pests

ALTHOUGH described earlier as a good food, cyclops can also come under the heading of Pests where very small newly-hatched fry of certain egg-laying fishes are concerned. If many of them are present they will definitely clear a whole spawn of such fry as neons, rosy tetras etc., but this of course concerns only those aquarists who are going in for fish breeding.

There are other pests that the beginner may occasionally come across. They may be introduced to the tank with live foods caught from ponds, or from plants which have not been thoroughly washed before being placed in the aquarium. The majority of these pests are large enough to see, and can easily be removed before they have done much damage.

HYDRA are deadly to small fry below $\frac{1}{4}''$ in length, and although the beginner may think that as his fishes are $1''$ or more long, hydra need not worry him, this is only half true, because hydra will divide and quickly infest a tank, sticking to the plants, rocks and glass, and looking most unsightly. Moreover, if daphnia or similar foods are fed into this tank the hydra, once they have become numerous, will soon take the majority of this food and the fishes will get only a small portion. There is no point in feeding pests; therefore they will have to be removed. Unfortunately, hydra when contracted are not much larger than daphnia, but they can expand and then become nearly $1''$ in length overall. The creature is greyish-brown in colour and somewhat resembles a tree in winter. It has a trunk and several long tentacles waving about at the top. These tentacles are forever searching for food, and as soon as one touches a daphnia or very small fish it paralyses it with stinging cells. The tentacle then curves inwards, and the victim is passed into the central mouth. But the hydra is not content with such a small feed. Even whilst the first victim is being swallowed the other tentacles are waving in search of extra prey, many of them being successful at the same time.

Although the creature has no legs it can move quite a long distance in a very short time. This it does by bending over, gripping with its tentacles, letting go with the sucker foot, and moving itself half-an-inch or so. Upon repeating this action it does not take it long to move to another place where the food supply may be more plentiful. Hydra reproduces mostly by budding, the baby one budding from the side of the trunk, much like a new shoot on a rosebush. If the creature is decapitated it is quite likely for the two halves now separated to bud independently; so it may be seen that reproduction is fairly rapid.

Many books state that large blue gouramis will devour hydra, but the beginner with a community tank is unlikely to have large blue gouramis as these fish grow to 4″ in length and are somewhat pugnacious. Moreover, the blue gourami usually takes a feed of hydra only when extremely hungry, and a good aquarist does not keep his fishes in such a state. One teaspoonful of vinegar to each gallon of water will make life unpleasant for the hydra, but some seem to survive. This cure makes the water more acid, and is not particularly recommended.

Limnia stagnalis, the common pond snail, is an excellent hydra eater. It will travel over sand, rocks, plants and glass, slicing a hydra off at the base with its sharp scythe-like tongue. These snails are common enough in any artificial pond and should not be difficult to obtain. Since they are in cool water when living in ponds, they should be floated in a jam-jar for one hour in the aquarium, so that the temperature slowly rises before they are tipped out into the tank. After they have done their work and all the hydra have disappeared, it is as well to remove them before they lay too many eggs on the plants. Keep them in a covered battery jar outside, feeding them occasionally with dried food. Here they will breed, and more will be ready if wanted on another occasion.

A very effective cure for hydra is to pass a weak electric current through the water. This may be done by a 4-volt battery (obtainable quite cheaply at most garages), and attaching to each terminal a length of insulated wire. The wires run over the top of the aquarium, and enter the water at opposite ends. The insulation is bared back 1″, and the wire attached to a penny or small square of copper. This acts as two poles and the electric current will make its way through the water from one pole to the other. In an hour or two the hydra will begin to look very sick, and if careful watch is kept some may be seen to flop over like a withered tree, lose the grip with their sucker foot, and fall dead to the bottom of the tank. The current has no effect, even on small fry. However, once the hydra have been killed in, say, six hours, it is better to remove the wires as copper in water is a cumulative poison.

PLANARIA WORMS: These are flat brown-grey worms about $\frac{1}{16}''$ wide, and from $\frac{1}{4}''$ to $\frac{1}{2}''$ long. Some have a diamond-shaped head. They are death to fry, but harmless to fishes 1" or so in length. Nevertheless, a tank infested with them is unsightly, and they will devour much of the food fed to the fishes. At the same time they will be using up oxygen and adding to the carbon dioxide present in the water.

If a small piece of meat about $\frac{1}{2}''$ in diameter is left in the tank overnight, many of the planarias will gather on it and it may be removed in the early morning and destroyed. Any planarias still seen moving about on the glass should be wiped upwards with a finger until they are out of the water. They will then stick to the finger and can be destroyed.

If the tank is really infested with planaria worms it is usually quicker to take it down, scrape all the sides, and wash out with salty water. The planaria will be plentiful in the sand, so this must be scalded with very hot water and stirred until all the planaria are killed. The plants should be washed thoroughly under a running tap, and afterwards it is a help to place them first in slightly warm, and then in very cold water alternately. The temperature changes cause a shock to the system of the planaria, which let go and fall to the bottom of the basin. The plants can then be tipped into water in which a small amount of vinegar has been poured; or alternatively in which a very few grains of potassium permanganate have been allowed to dissolve, making the water a cherry pink colour. Do not leave the plants in this for long, half-an-hour at most, or they will be stained brown and seriously set back, or very probably killed.

LEECHES: Leeches are large enough to be seen quickly,

usually about 1″ to 1½″ long and possibly ⅛″ thick. They may attach themselves to fishes and attempt to suck their blood. When seen they should be picked out and destroyed. They are not common, and in all probability the aquarist will never see one.

WATER TIGERS are occasionally seen. They are usually collected with live food such as daphnia, cyclops etc. They are a greenish-yellow in colour, have long pointed bodies with six legs at the chest end, and the head has two sharp pincers protruding forward from it. With these the tiger seizes a small fish and proceeds to suck the blood and juice from the fish. It has to rise to the surface tail foremost to breathe, and that is the reason it is often caught in daphnia nets. If live food is placed in an enamel basin, as recommended earlier, tigers may easily be seen and picked out. Small ones up to ¼″ in length will probably be eaten by the fishes, but larger ones 1″ to 1½″ in length can be very dangerous.

DRAGONFLY LARVAE: These are very occasionally collected when catching daphnia. They are long, thick creatures with enormous jaws. They are particularly dangerous because they can approach a victim, and when half-an-inch away suddenly project their jaws forward and grasp their prey. All are large enough to be seen and should be removed at once.

There are of course other pests, but few are likely to be met with in the average aquarium. It must be remembered that the domestic cat has been known to put its paw into an uncovered tank and occasionally hook out a fish; and terrapins should never be placed in an aquarium as these will attempt to catch a fish.

INSECTICIDES: can be classified under pests, for few people realise that these sprays are deadly. If fruit trees are sprayed out of doors make sure that the windows of the room in which the tank is situated are shut. Similarly, do not use a push-button fly-spray containing pybuthrin near the fish tank. If this settles on the water it can have disastrous effects upon the fish. If it is absolutely necessary to spray round the fish tank, cover it with a cloth or blanket temporarily, and when the flies have been killed the windows should be opened before the cloth covering the aquarium is removed.

SNAILS. Although many books recommend snails in the aquarium, the author regards most snails as pests. In the past a wrong impression has arisen about them. Many beginners believe that they will eat fish excreta and thereby keep the tank clean. This is quite erroneous. No snails will eat fish excreta. On the contrary, they will add their own to that already present. True, they will eat particles of food that the fishes have missed, or which have become slightly unfresh and which the fishes no longer fancy; but this goes to show that the fishes are being over-fed and, as pointed out earlier in this book, this is bad aquarium management.

It is equally true that snails will eat some algae, but they do not go over the glass like a lawn-mower, cleaning it all in one session. They will make trails here and there, but not touch the algae on either side of these trails. Here again an extensive growth of algae shows poor aquarium management. There should be little or none of it, in which case the snails will not be required to eat it.

Where snails are introduced, despite this warning, a little extra food will have to be given in order that they may eat. They are prolific breeders, laying eggs on the rocks, undersides of plant leaves etc. and can soon become a nuisance. The little physa snail, which is small, hard and nearly black, is rarely attacked by the fishes. Thus reproduction goes on unhindered, and in time it may be necessary to take down the tank, thoroughly cleanse it, scald the sand etc. The beginner is almost bound to have a few snails hatching out from eggs which are adhering to the plants that he buys, but as soon as any snails reach a recognisable size and are in a convenient position near the front glass to be removed, this should be done.

If the aquarist is vigilant in the first fortnight he will remove all the snails before they are large enough to breed, and may then be untroubled. Most snails have a bad habit of biting at the plant leaves, and can ruin a specimen plant by puncturing the leaves all over with ugly holes. Worse than this, they do not confine themselves to the leaves but bite through the stems lower down. The whole leaf either withers, or is detached and floats to the surface of the water to rot.

Other snails that are a nuisance are (1) The ramshorn snail. This is a flat round snail, rather the shape of a thick washer. It may be red or black, and although the red-shelled ones look attractive they really are a pest. Even if one wants to keep a few red snails in a tank, very often the fishes will attack and kill them. They then lie on the sand and putrefy. However, once established they breed prolifically, and fishes seem to tire of them and no longer attack them. Getting rid of them then becomes a major operation.

(2) The Malayan snail, which has a long pointed cone, rather like the 'horn of plenty', scavenges deep in the sand, and during daytime is rarely seen. It comes out at night and swarms all over the aquarium. This snail is not such a pest, but few aquarists realise how many they have in their tanks until they come down in the early hours of the morning, shine a torch on the tank and see several hundreds. Whether they are deliberately kept or not, every now and then they should be thoroughly thinned out.

APPLE SNAILS. There are several varieties of apple snails. *Ampullaria cuprina* has its uses, but only to the aquarist who intends to breed and rear egg-laying fishes in large numbers continually. These snails eat lettuce leaves and may bite through the normal aquarium plants. Their droppings form an excellent medium in which infusoria (*see* p. 68) can breed and multiply, but to the aquarist with one tank they are unnecessary.

SIX

Diseases

TROPICAL FISH are not, luckily, subject to a great number of diseases. In fact, if they are well cared for and kept in clean healthy tanks at the normal temperature, if new plants are washed thoroughly before being placed in the aquarium, and new fishes thoroughly quarantined before being added to the tank, there is no reason why they should contract or spread any disease.

WHITE SPOT: Probably the commonest disease amongst tropical fishes is white spot. It is caused by a parasite which burrows beneath the scales of the fish. The spot grows to about the size of a thin needle pushed through a piece of paper, and forms a cyst, opaque white in colour. When ripe, this cyst falls off the fish and settles on the sand. Here it bursts open, and anything from 500 to 2,000 of the parasites are released. These swim around in search of a new host. Many are unable to do this and die, but sufficient reach their goal, and the disease continues and multiplies all the time.

All fishes purchased should be quarantined in an unplanted tank for at least ten days. During this time it is as well to give them a mild treatment, since prevention is better than cure. If they look perfectly healthy after this period it is safe to place them in the aquarium. Now, a fish that has been in contact with white spot may have one or two parasites on it, but they will not have had time to encyst. Thus a fish which does not have white spots on it is not necessarily free of the disease. The spots may develop three to five days later, and if that fish has been placed in the tank, even if taken out immediately, some of the cysts will have fallen off, and the parasites will then be free-swimming in the water, and will soon attack other fishes.

In the past it has been thought that White Spot was caused solely by a chill, on the grounds that the mucus which covers all fishes' scales is thinned or destroyed, and the parasites ever present in the water are able to get between and under the scales. This is not strictly true, because if a fish with White Spot is placed with other healthy fishes which have not been subjected to any chill whatever, they are more than likely to contract the disease within five days. On the other hand, a healthy fish which does suffer a sudden chill by mistakenly being placed into some much cooler water can often be netted out and returned to the aquarium, and still not be attacked by White Spot. The majority of cases where the disease occurs is because infected fish are introduced into the tank. This warning should be taken very seriously. To the aquarist who has only one tank buying a second one may be very well worth while, and less than the loss incurred with fish that have been kept for a year and grown to breeding size only to be attacked by this disease.

There are various treatments. Mercurochrome is one, quinine sulphate is another. With the former add four drops of 2% solution to each gallon of water, and with the latter add about three grains to the gallon. However, the author considers that mercurochrome if used more than once is apt to stunt the growth of the fishes; and quinine sulphate if used too strongly can cause their death.

Methylene blue seems to be entirely safe. It is very cheap, and can be bought at most chemists in a 4% aqueous solution. Sufficient should be added to the water with an eye dropper to turn it a deep dark blue. At this strength it will have a serious effect upon some of the weaker plants; so if a spare tank is available it is better to place all the fishes in that tank without plants and treat them there. To the beginner the deep dark blue will appear frightening, but it will do no harm whatsoever to the scaled fishes. In fact many of them look fitter and in better colour when they come out than ever they did before they went in. After eight to ten days, if the solution is strong enough, the fishes will be cured and may be returned to their proper home. All the protozoa that were left free swimming in the aquarium will not have found a host on which to thrive and will have starved and died, so a new attack will not take place.

Methylene blue can often be used as a preventive, but in this case it need only be used as a pale blue solution. At this strength it may be used in a planted tank, and a few days later the water in the tank will begin to clear. This strength of solution sometimes helps in clearing green water, as the blue dye destroys the tiny green cells of algae.

VELVET is another disease that can be brought in from non-quarantined fishes; in fact it may develop for no particular reason at all, often attacking young fishes when about one-third grown. The spots are very much smaller, and are more of a dusty brown colour. They are also very much closer together. Fishes badly affected will soon have their tails smothered, and the trailing edge will become ragged and slowly disintegrate. A fish viewed head on will appear to be covered in a brownish powder over its back.

The best treatment is plain salt. Add one level teaspoonful of ordinary cooking salt to each gallon of water. This is usually effective in forty-eight hours. If not, the dose should be repeated at half strength.

GILL FLUKES: This disease is rather rare. It is caused by a flat worm parasite, Gyrodactylus, which lodges in the skin and especially in the gills. The irritation caused brings about a lymph covering the gill membranes, so that these organs are unable to extract the dissolved oxygen so easily from the water. The fish is unable to breathe properly and performs weak spiral movements in the water. Usually all the fishes are infected within a short period.

Tablets of one of the flavins such as Euflavin, Acriflavin, Tripa-flavin etc. are effective. Use one tablet, i.e. approximately 1·75 grains to each twenty gallons of water. The tablet, or half tablet, is simply placed in an old cup containing warm water, and when completely dissolved the liquid should be poured into the aquarium. It will turn the water a fluorescent greenish-yellow but should bring about a cure within thirty-six hours, after which time some of the water can be changed, and any fluorescent coloration remaining will gradually disappear.

FUNGUS is not usually a serious disease with tropical fishes, although it is one of the main troubles with cold water fishes. This is because the fungus thrives better in cold water than warm; but a tropical fish that has been bitten or badly damaged by another fish so that the scales are torn away can be attacked by fungus. The disease is not generally infectious, hence the patient can be isolated in a floating jam-jar to which has been added a level coffeespoonful of ordinary salt. It is better to change the salt water in the jam-jar daily until the fungus is completely cured.

There are two other very infectious and contagious diseases, called mouth fungus and saddleback.

MOUTH FUNGUS. Fishes with this disease appear as if they had a piece of cotton wool in the mouth, and as they breathe the fungus will move in and out.

With SADDLEBACK an opaque patch appears on the upper part of the caudal peduncle just in front of the tail. It soon spreads further, the opaque patch becoming dead flesh. The affected portions will rot away and drop off. Any other fish that bites this area is liable to contract the disease on the lips. Both this and mouth fungus spread rapidly, and if it has not gone too far the infected fishes had better be destroyed in the hope that they will not infect others. Nevertheless treatment must be started right away.

Ordinary salt appears to be the best cure. It has to be used at double the strength recommended for velvet. Even this will not be strong enough, and so for the first few days the strength must be built up and up so that the fishes get accustomed to it over a period. The effective dose would probably be too strong for them to take at one treatment. A cure will eventually be effected, but it must be understood that during this time many more fishes will contract the disease and most of these will die.

The disease will not break out spontaneously. It is introduced with newly imported fish. Therefore, irrespective of white spot and other diseases, a quarantine tank is really a necessity to prevent the spread of saddleback and mouth fungus.

There are a few other diseases but they are somewhat rare. A few may be brought about by the aquarist himself, in which case he has only himself to blame for neglect or bad management.

WASTING DISEASE. This appears to be a form of tuberculosis, and the fishes soon become thin and hollow-bellied. It is mostly caused by overcrowding and lack of oxygen.

SHIMMIES: With this ailment fishes remain in mid water and have an exaggerated shake from head to tail. It may be an infection of the gills and usually caused by overcrowding, and by fouling of the water. The best thing is to thin out the fishes, cleanse the water and give aeration for a period.

BOILS: These are usually blood disorders caused by bacteria, and frequently result from the feeding of tubifex worms to the fishes. As explained earlier, these worms inhabit filthy areas, and hence contain bacteria internally. The aquarist who persists in feeding tubifex must hold himself responsible.

DROPSY: A fish infected with dropsy becomes very swollen and the scales, which normally lie flat, stick out on edge. There is no certain cure. Placed in shallow water, to which has been added a teaspoonful of salt, may bring temporary relief, but in all probability the fish will not live longer than two or three months. It is not contagious and will not affect other fishes, although some of the Anabantids and Mollienisia seem to have an inherited tendency, but by no means all are affected.

NEON DISEASE: is thought to be a form of tuberculosis, though this is by no means sure. A whitish patch develops on the side, but is mostly internal, eventually completely breaking the blue line running along the flanks. There is no known cure, and the fish is best destroyed. The disease is said to attack Glowlight tetras occasionally, but the author has never known of a case. With neons it usually occurs in imported fish. Home-bred specimens at first seemed entirely free, but from personal experience it has been found that parent neon fish bred regularly every week for three or four months produce youngsters which rarely, if ever, show the disease. But if the same fish are bred for longer periods the youngsters appear to develop a weakness, and with each successive brood more and more of the progeny eventually become afflicted, say two in the first brood, twelve in the next, thirty in the next and so on.

Lastly, the wise aquarist will keep a small First Aid kit handy. This should contain salt, methylene blue, potassium permanganate, acriflavin tablets etc., all ready for an occasion when they are urgently required. With all treatments, the sooner they are started the better.

SEVEN

Transportation of Fishes

TROPICAL FISHES available for sale in this country are either those which are bred in fish hatcheries in England, or imported from abroad. Home-bred specimens generally have some advantages over the imported ones. They do not have to endure so much handling and carriage. Usually the breeder wholesales his fish to Pet Shops and they in turn sell them to the public; whereas imported fishes are caught in the wild, carried for many miles, maybe in tins, on the heads of natives to a base where they are either sold to local exporters, or in some cases shipped direct to England, America, and the Continent. Far Eastern fish may pass through importers' hands in England on their way to America; whereas the fishes from the western hemisphere may be flown to Florida, thence to New York, and then on to England and the continent. Thus they pass through more hands, and frequently during the forced stages on their journey are tipped into tanks of varying waters. They are usually crowded together, and disease may break out because of all these varying conditions.

This necessitates treatment at different stages on the way. Such chemicals as terramycin, copper sulphate, salt etc. are often placed in the water to prevent, or stop, the spread of disease. This may result in fishes arriving in poor condition, thin from lack of food, and in some cases nearly sterile from immersion in various chemicals.

Home-bred fish have a much shorter and easier travel, and are much less likely to arrive thin, weak and diseased.

Fishes bred and raised in our own waters, although they vary in different localities, are at least fishes that are tank-raised and used to captivity. Some aquarists insist that they are superior in every way. There are some species which so far cannot be bred in captivity, and therefore foreign importations have to be relied upon. In a few cases there are species which lack something in the aquarium that they got in wild life, and these do not reach full maturity, and consequently do not breed. Here again wild importations are essential. New species are continually being found, and naturally these come from the wild. The fish hatcheries do their best to obtain some of the specimens, study them and attempt to breed them. If successful, time will show whether these are superior or inferior to the original wild ones.

Many amateurs have more than one tank and breed fishes. Some of these enthusiasts are quite willing to exchange fish with each other, but they rarely have sufficient numbers of various specimens to supply the trade. Thus the trade depends upon the fish hatcheries, and upon importations. In the olden days the fishes were shipped in large round shallow cans. This shape was necessary to ensure as large a surface area as possible. Even so, four or five gallons of water were necessary in each can, making the weight nearly $\frac{1}{2}$-cwt. Into this were put perhaps 50 to a 100 fishes, according to size. These cans had perforated lids so that oxygen could enter and carbon dioxide escape. In the loading and unloading many were tipped up and in some cases all the water lost. The fishes would die once their gills became dry. Although oxygen was able to enter the water, if the fishes were overcrowded the build-up of carbon dioxide gas was so great that many deaths followed. The cans were shipped on transport vessels, and many of these were equipped with aerators and specially warmed compartments. Even so, the journey might take anything from a fortnight to three weeks or more. Also, the weight of water made transportation expensive.

To-day wild fishes are placed into plastic bags, and instead of 50-100, each bag (roughly 18″ in diameter, and 2′ high) contains about 500 fishes. Yet they are in perhaps only half a gallon to one gallon of water. Immediately the warmed water is put in the bag and the fishes placed into it, the air is squeezed out of the bag and it is blown up with pure oxygen from a compressed oxygen cylinder.

It must be remembered that atmospheric air is four-fifths nitrogen and one-fifth oxygen; but now the bags contain no nitrogen, but only oxygen. Thus there is a large supply of this gas free to dissolve in the water as the fishes require it.

The neck of the bag is now twisted round, bent over and tied securely. The bag or bags are then placed in large cardboard boxes which are insulated with hay or crumpled newspaper in an attempt to reduce heat losses. Space is booked on aeroplanes and they are loaded into warmed cabins. Their travel from the Far East instead of taking weeks is now reduced to hours. The small weight of water, and the greater number of fishes in each bag, make transportation charges considerably less.

Even in these days when the prices of most commodities are rising the cost of fishes is continually dropping. Many beginners are under the impression that tropical fishes are liable to be very expensive. The majority cost less than a packet of cigarettes; and if they live for two years one can hardly consider them expensive luxuries.

Whether the aquarist buys his fish from a hatchery, a Pet Shop, or from a friend, and does not have to travel a great distance, he may carry his fishes home in screw-top jars. Many aquarists make themselves wooden boxes with a hinged lid, complete with handle. The case is lined with asbestos or foam rubber, and fitted with compartments to hold three or four shallow sweet-jars. The shape of the jars, and the insulation in the box, ensure that the fishes will have plenty of oxygen and the heat will be retained whilst being transported home, whether by train, bus or private car.

In some cases the aquarist buying fish from a Pet Shop may have them handed to him in a small plastic bag. Although the fish will have plenty of oxygen, unless this bag is placed in a cardboard box insulated with crumpled newspaper, heat loss will be rapid. The fish hatcheries in this country that send regular supplies to the Pet Shops use plastic bags blown up with oxygen, and these are put in insulated cardboard boxes, taken to the main line terminal and despatched by passenger train, the shopkeeper being notified of the time of arrival. He is expected to meet the train and take the fish back to his shop as quickly as possible.

The main thing to remember is that when transporting fishes, even short distances, they need plenty of oxygen. Wide-necked thermos flasks, jars or plastic bags are the most suitable, and these should be filled not more than two-thirds full of water. They then need to be placed in some container that will retain the warmth as long as possible.

CLUBS

In this little book it is impossible to give all the information one would wish regarding the keeping and breeding of tropical fishes. But if it encourages anybody to start this fascinating hobby, and to maintain a community tank in good condition for a year or two, it will have achieved its object. By then the beginner will know the main principles, and may be anxious to learn more.

There are several aquarists' magazines published, some for the trade, some for individuals. There are at least two in England, and others are received from abroad. The English ones generally give the names and addresses of club secretaries; but if these are omitted occasionally, any individual can write to the editor and be informed of his nearest aquarists' club. For a small subscription, varying between 2/6d and perhaps 5/- per annum he can become a member.

Such local clubs usually hold monthly meetings, and at these meetings club members may give talks about their experiences. On more special nights a good lecturer is booked, and members may listen to an expert with vast experience. At other times there may be a lecture with slides, or even a film to watch. A beginner may learn to avoid disastrous mistakes without actually experiencing them himself.

With regard to breeding fishes, instead of having to experiment with various types of water at different pH values and different degrees of hardness, he may take advantage of what he learns; and instead of pioneering all the way himself, he can jump miles on the road to success. Therefore joining a club may be well worth the small cost. In addition he may make friends with people of similar interests, visit their houses, see their fishes, and frequently be given some fishes by another aquarist who has bred the specimens and now has too many.

All the same, people joining a club should not do so entirely because of what they can gain. They should be ready to give a hand and help in the general running of the club, perhaps organize a Christmas show, and be willing to help those with less knowledge than themselves.

Clubs quite frequently hold table shows. Members bring along in screw-topped sweet jars specimen fish that they think are in superb condition and good colour. These are judged and prizes are awarded. This prize may be only a small show card; but the first show card one receives marked 'First Prize' gives a tremendous fillip to any aquarist. In an area where there are several clubs there may be inter-club shows where one can match one's fishes, not only against one's own members, but also against members of other clubs in the vicinity. To win a first prize here proves that one is keeping healthy and particularly fine specimens.

After inter-club shows there may be area shows, and then county shows. Some of these shows are for individual fishes, for breeders' classes, for furnished aquaria, and club entries. Then there are national shows in which one can compete with other aquarists from all over the British Isles. Here the first prize may be a silver cup, a plaque, or a national card, which is a great credit to anyone who holds it. Finally there are international shows, in which entrants from several countries compete. Of course if the show is held abroad the individual will either have to pay his fare, or he may be able to arrange to send his entry with others from a club.

EIGHT

Anatomy of Fishes

ALTHOUGH everybody knows what a fish looks like, few people really bother to examine them closely. They are highly complex creatures and, like human beings, contain most of the same organs. Without going too closely into a fish's structure, a brief description of the main organs may be helpful.

The body is covered with skin and bony plates or scales. Each scale overlaps the one behind, not only to offer protection, but to help the streamlining and the fish's speed through the water. Some fishes are elongated in shape, and the majority compressed laterally. The Angel fish, for instance, has a circular body 3" or 4" in diameter, but from side to side is barely ¼". (A plaice is much the same, but lies over on one side.)

Most fishes have seven fins (*see* Fig. 2), one on the back, known as the dorsal; two underneath the belly, known as the ventral fins; one underneath, mid-way between these fins and the tail, known as the anal fin; the tail, known as the caudal fin, and two each side of the forward portion of the body, known as the pectoral fins.

The pectoral fins compare with the forelegs of an animal or the arms of a man; the ventral fins are the hindlegs. The dorsal fin is sometimes split into two portions, the foremost being called the anterior dorsal, and the hindmost the posterior dorsal. A few fishes have, behind the dorsal fin, a small fatty fin called the adipose fin.

The dorsal is usually large, and stands up because of the hard bony rays it contains, though these are often more rigid in the forward portion. This fin can be raised or lowered for display in courtship, or as a menacing gesture to frighten away an adversary. The rear portion can be moved to the right or left, and helps to steer the fish when speeding along.

The pectoral fins are used for paddling when the fish is turning

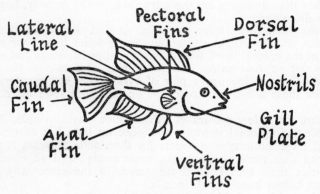

Fig. 2. Firemouth Cichlid

on its axis, and for planing up and down when swimming to the surface or diving to the bottom. The ventral fins act as stabilisers, and many modern ships have now adopted this principle to prevent or reduce roll. The anal fin in live-bearing fishes changes shape in adult specimens, and becomes a breeding organ. It also helps to keep the fish upright, and is an aid in steering.

The tail fin is the main means of propulsion. One stroke of this powerful fin can drive a fish many times its own length at high speed through the water.

Fishes have mouths, and many of them have sharp teeth just inside with which to bite and tear off animal or vegetable food. Other fishes have bony plates in the throat with which they grind food small enough to be swallowed.

Nostrils: Above the mouth are two small holes which are the fish's nostrils, so that it is possible for fishes to smell things, even under water. Sharks and piranhas are well-known examples of fishes that are attracted by the smell of blood.

Ears: The ears of fish are internal. Most of the sounds picked up are probably more related to wave lengths and vibrations than the tonal qualities; but recently experiments have shown that shoals of fishes can be attracted by music played under water; but whether the vibrations are the attraction, or the melody, has yet to be discovered.

Eyes: Most fishes have two eyes, so that they can see their enemies and find their way about. Some fishes have four eyes, such as the mudskippers, which live in shallowish water and often climb out on mud banks. The lower pair of eyes scan the surrounding water; the upper pair of eyes search the surrounding air, for these fishes will come out on land and seize insects as food.

There are a few species of fishes which have no eyes. They inhabit underground streams, and since no light has ever penetrated these subterranean waters for thousands of years Nature decreed that these organs were unnecessary; and so over the centuries their eyes have disappeared, in the same way that human beings have lost their tails.

Fishes with eyes do not have eyelids, so it is cruel to switch on the electric light over their tank after a period of total darkness. The sudden illumination causes fishes to dash hither and thither to get out of the light, and they may damage themselves against the walls of the aquarium. Before switching on the aquarium lights, the room light should be put on at least five minutes earlier, so that the effect is gradual. Similarly, turn the tank hood light off five minutes before turning off the room light, so that they are not suddenly plunged from brilliant light into total darkness.

Gills: have already been mentioned earlier in this book. They are protected by the bony plate known as the gill plate, and the soft membranes underneath contain blood-vessels which extract the dissolved oxygen from the water entering the fish's mouth and afterwards expelled through the gill slits. Many people believe that a fish taken out of water will die immediately. This is not so, provided the gills are kept wet. They are then able to extract oxygen present in the air for a prolonged period.

Lateral line: Along each side of a fish can be seen a very thin line. This starts just behind the gill plates and may rise a short distance to drop again mid-way along its length, and then finish in a more or less straight line through to the tail. It is only in certain lights that this line is distinguishable. It then looks as if the fish has been scraped with a needle. This line is called the lateral line, and is of the utmost importance.

The lateral line is made up of canals which contain sense organs developed in the skin. Vibrations in the water are picked up by the cells and passed through to the swim bladder, which acts as an auxiliary hearing organ. It is thought that fishes can recognise their own species from the wavelengths picked up by the lateral line, much as an aerial picks up radio soundwaves. Similarly, they are able to recognise large dangerous fishes which are approaching too closely, and take evasive action. Certainly the blind Cave tetra, which has no eyes, is able to detect objects such as plants, other fishes, rocks, and the walls of the aquarium, before bumping into them; a very slight turn and the fish glides by without knocking against anything.

The vent is situated just in front of the anal fin, and waste products of food are excreted here. In close proximity is the *cloaca*, which is the urinary and genital duct.

Internal organs: Fishes have a heart, liver, kidneys, intestines, testes, ova etc. There is not sufficient space to go fully into all these. However, one feature should be mentioned. This is the *swim bladder*. It enables fish to rise and sink, or stay balanced in mid-water without any effort. It operates rather like the ballast tanks of submarines, or the gas container of a balloon. The more gas there is in the container, the more the balloon will rise. When the gas is let out, the balloon will begin to sink. Fishes are able to fill or discharge the amount of gas in the swim bladder, and so do not have to battle with their fins all the time in order to maintain a certain level.

NINE

Live-Bearing Fishes

TROPICAL FISHES can broadly be divided into two categories, the live-bearers and the egg-layers. Apparently it is very surprising to most people who have not kept tropical fishes that there are species which give birth to live young and do not lay eggs, but this is a fact. Live-bearers will be dealt with first, partly because most beginners find them fairly easy to keep, and even to breed, and partly because there are not so many of them.

Sexing is easy, as the male's gonopodium is easily distinguishable from the female's anal fin. At birth both fishes look the same, but as the males grow older the front rays of the anal fin get longer and thicker, and the remaining rays shrink almost away. This leaves him with a rodlike organ normally pointed backwards, but it can be moved sideways or forwards at will (*see* Fig. 3). The female's fin remains the normal fan shape which everyone expects.

When mating the male darts round the female with his fins spread, courting her, and donning his finest colours. He may dart forwards and backwards, but eventually approaches the female from behind, and with the gonopodium pointing forwards and slightly to one side, inserts the tip into the vent of the female. Spermatozoa are injected and the eggs fertilised internally. The female at this stage of her life is usually larger than the male and slightly deeper bodied. Just above and in front of her ventral fin may be seen a clear or darkish patch known as the gravid spot (*see* Fig. 3). It is in this sac that the fertilised eggs are carried and, fed by the mother's bloodstream, begin to develop. The abdomen of the female grows larger and the gravid spot more extensive. If very close watch is kept the eyes of the baby fishes may be seen through the thin walls of the sac. At birth, roughly a month after mating, the young are born and are expelled one by one, very often tail first. A young female may bear anything from ten to

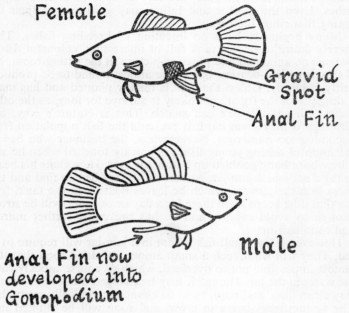

Fig. 3. Live-bearers, 'Mollienisia'

twenty-five babies, but as she gets older some species may give birth to over 200 youngsters in one brood.

There is another curious fact which the uninitiated do not know about live-bearers, and that is that the female is capable of carrying and storing spermatazoa from the male fish. If after the original mating she never sees another male she may still produce four or even five broods at monthly intervals until all the sperms are used up.

The baby fish when born are about ¼" long. They sink in the water to lodge amongst the plants or fall to the sand, where they lie motionless until they have had a short time to gain a little strength. Then they make short darts from one spot to another.

Instinct warns them that they are very liable to be eaten by bigger fishes. Even the mother and father may gulp any of their offspring that come their way.

Many beginners have no intention of breeding fishes. They merely desire to have a tank full of interesting, colourful fish to provide an animated and pleasing picture in the sitting-room; but if they keep live-bearers, babies are almost bound to be produced fairly regularly. Unless the tank is thickly planted and has many hiding places the fry are not likely to survive for long, as the other fishes will eat all they can snatch. This is Nature's way, and although it may seem hard, it prevents the fish population from becoming too numerous. Nevertheless, the beginner who has no intention of raising young fishes is quickly touched when he sees a new-born baby gobbled up before his eyes. He softens his heart, grabs a net and a jam-jar, gathers all the fry he can find and tips them into the jam-jar, which he leaves floating in the tank, feeling that if he keeps them there for a day or two they will be strong enough to avoid capture and he has prevented further murder and cannibalism.

However, a few small fishes kept in a jam-jar will require to be fed. They will want such a small amount of dried food that it is almost impossible not to overfeed, which of course quickly fouls the water in the jar. Though it may be changed it does not usually stay clean long, and requires to be changed practically every day. The young fishes begin to grow, and soon will be stunted in a small jam-jar. They need room to exercise, and more oxygen to feed the muscles through the bloodstream. Within a week they will require a bigger jar. They will probably have to reach an age of one month to six weeks before they are large enough to be turned out into the aquarium and be safe from the other fishes. If these are large the babies may have to remain segregated for perhaps three months.

In the meantime other female live-bearers in the tank will probably have produced youngsters, and by now the tank of the soft-hearted aquarist will be full of floating jam-jars containing young in various stages of development. Although a few babies can be raised in this manner, one is unlikely to be able to raise a fair stock without other tanks being brought into use.

The beginner must remember that the fishes that produce young regularly in his tank will produce young just as easily in other aquarists' tanks, and thus they become commonplace, and it is not easy to sell those species which can so easily be bred by others. However, superb specially line-bred fishes will always find a market, and the breeder wishing to reproduce these specimens will do well to have several more tanks. He will require a breeding tank approximately 24" long × 8" × 8". If plants are used it must be thoroughly planted, receive the right amount of light, and be kept at about 78°F.

When the female is about to deliver she is taken out from the main tank and placed in the breeding tank, so that a few days later her brood is delivered there. She may try to eat a few of her own young, but planted thickets will prevent much of this, and immediately after the complete brood has been born she is caught again and replaced in her original tank. The babies are now safe, and can be fed with microworm and fine dried food. They have sufficient space to grow to a length of $\frac{3}{4}$", and the greater volume of water is not so easily fouled.

In about a month's time they will need to be transferred to a larger tank, which is often called a ' growing on ' tank. This should be 36" long × 10" × 10", and will house them until they reach 1" or $1\frac{1}{4}$" in length. They can then be transferred to larger tanks for keeping or selling.

If they are to be line-bred fishes, as soon as the first signs of sexing appear the males will have to be separated from the females. The best female is probably mated back to the best original male, or vice versa. The best young male, if better than his father, may be mated back to his mother. Records must be kept, and only the best fish bred. The others are discarded, or sold cheaply.

For producing different colorations Mendel's Laws of Inheritance come into practice. This is quite a complicated study and beyond the scope of this book; but other books can be bought which will explain the theory to those who wish to produce a new coloured fish. Those who go in for producing new colours and hybrids will need to specialise in this type of breeding. It is practically impossible to do this and ordinary breeding at the same time.

Traps: Traps have been designed in plastic, glass and stainless steel wire mesh. Some float, others are attached by hooks to the top rim of the aquarium, and others will stand on legs in shallow tanks. These traps are placed in bare tanks containing only water (heater and thermostat, of course). The female about to deliver young is placed therein and the tank is covered by a sheet of glass. Outside the trap can be placed plenty of pieces of floating plant. These should be natural floating plants with their roots hanging down, or stems of other plants which will lie horizontally in the water. When the babies are born they will be able to go through the small mesh of the trap, and instinct makes them hide in the safety of the plants. The mother of course is unable to get through the small mesh, so cannot follow and swallow them.

When the whole brood is born she is caught and replaced in her original tank, and the trap is removed. Provided the tank is large enough, the babies will thrive without any sand or plants in it. Careful watch must be kept not to foul it, and the babies moved on when they require more space.

SPECIES OF LIVE-BEARERS

The following species are listed and described as being most suitable for the beginner.

Glarydichthys falcates. This is an attractive little fish, males about 1″ long, females 1¼″. They are a pale goldish colour, and have a bright blue iris encircling the pupil of the eye. They are peaceful, not too common, will take all the usual foods mentioned in Chapter 4.

Heterandria formosa, (the mosquito fish). This is the smallest of the live-bearers, males reaching a length of only ¾″, females 1¼″. The overall colour is olive brown, but a dark stripe runs along the sides from nose to tail, and a black spot appears in the dorsal and anal fins. The fish is peaceful, but owing to its small size, particularly during its early life, really requires to be raised in a separate tank. Otherwise larger fishes may devour and reduce the stocks to almost nil. It produces its young over a longer period than do most other live-bearers, a few babies being born one day and a few of the next. It will take any small food.

Lebistes reticulatus, (the guppy). Probably still the favourite fish of most aquarists. The males are extremely colourful, being splashed with red, blue, green, yellow and various shades and mixtures. No two males are exactly alike. The average length is about 1⅛″. The females are a plain sandy grey and reach a length of 1½″-1¾″. The ordinary plain guppy is worth little. They reproduce regularly, five or six broods a year being not uncommon. Simply because there are so many about, the price has dropped to practically nothing; but had they never been seen before they would easily fetch £1 each.

Guppies have been line-bred by experts, and these experts have produced truly magnificent fish. Some, called *Veil tails*, have a tail as long as the body, widening as it extends in a huge V, and the trailing edge from top to bottom may be nearly 1″ in length. This is splashed with gorgeous colours, and even the females to-day have coloured dorsals and colour in the caudal fin. Fine examples will still fetch 50/- to £3 per pair.

Then there are *Scarf tails*, with long tails rather like a streamer of coloured ribbon; *Sword tails* in which the lower rays of the tail extend beyond the rest in a backward-pointing sword; *Double Sword tails* where the sword extends from both the top and bottom edges of the tail fin.

There are many other shapes of tails, and there are as well various coloured guppies: *Gold guppies*, still carrying the splashes of colour overlaid on a gold background; *Lace guppies*, in which a network of black circles enclosing various colours gives the appearance of a network over the fish. Here again, all the various coloured types are hard to mention as new ones are being produced every year. These guppies may range from 6d to 30/- each according to type, colour, breeding etc. They are very peaceful, easily fed, and a joy in almost every community tank.

Limia. There are two species, *L. melanogaster* and *L. nigrofasciata*. The former is a smallish fish, males 1½″, females 1¾″. The body is blue, spangled with bright blue dots, the dorsal and tail fins being adorned with crescents of blue, black and yellow. The males are very active, darting hither and thither about the aquarium in pursuit of females. Takes any food.

The latter species is a golden colour traversed by thin vertical black bars. It is known as the Humpbacked Limia, as males on reaching maturity develop an arched back. This is not a deformity but a natural shape. The adult males grow a rather large dorsal fin and this is speckled with black. Will take any food. Though it reproduces quite easily, the females are inclined to eat their young. Trapping is recommended.

Mollienisia. Mollies are extremely peaceful. The original mollie was a greenish colour but, again through line-breeding, the Perma-black mollie has been produced. This is a velvety jet black all over, and may be of two species, *M. latipinna*, which has a some-what tall, long, wedge-shaped dorsal fin, length $2\frac{1}{2}''$-3", and *M. sphenops*, which has a short, round dorsal fin. Although a funereal black would not at first appear to be beautiful, this fish swimming against bright green plants is a sight not to be forgotten. Also their solid hue tends to show up the brighter colours of some of the other fishes by contrast. Length $2\frac{1}{2}''$-3".

There is still a third species, *M. velifera*. This is the king of mollies, and adult males may reach 5" in length. The dorsal fin is so large that it has been termed a sail fin. It will cover most of the fish's back in length, and when erected the front rays will stand up $1\frac{1}{4}''$ in height. The females are a little smaller, and their dorsal fins are not so grand, but still large. The fish is greenish in colour, has red spots on the body, dorsal and caudal fins, and there are rows of regular gold dots traversing the flanks from gill plate to tail.

Occasionally one comes across a sail fin mollie, usually pro-duced by crossing *M. velifera* and *M. latipinna*, and the resulting progeny crossed again and so on, until a Sail fin black occurs. Perhaps only 1 in 500 may develop this large fin, but he will be a prize fish. Unfortunately, the strain is not fixed and he will throw few, if any, sons that are jet black, and have the enormous black dorsal fin edged on its upper border by a thin line of red and gold.

Mollies like a high temperature, preferably 80°F. Their lips are situated on the upper part of the mouth as if slightly upturned. They like dried food, which they eat from the surface of the water, and prefer six or seven small feeds a day rather than one or two larger ones. In fact, to get big fish they have to be practically non-stop eaters. They like plenty of space, and browse most of the time, when dried food is not available, on algae. A plant that has become smothered with algae may be put in with the mollies,

8. *Hyphessobrycon rosaceous* (Rosy tetra)—Male (right) and Female

9. *Colisa lalia*
(Dwarf gourami)

). *Gyrinocheilus*
ymonieri
(Sucking loach)

Photo: Kathleen Cooke

11. *Tanichthys albonubes* (White cloud mountain minnow)

12. *Trichogaster leeri* (Lace gourami)

Photo: Kathleen Cooke

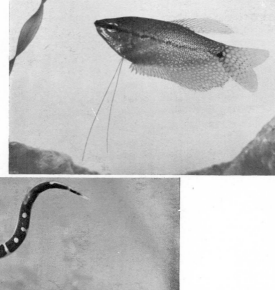

13. *Acanthophthalm semicinctus* (Kuhli E

Photo: Pace

who will pick it clean in a short while. To try to perform this by hand results in breaking pieces off the plant, or destroying it altogether.

Mollies occasionally suffer from a form of shimmies. They stay in mid-water, waggling violently from head to tail. This can often be cured by the addition of a teaspoonful of salt to each gallon of water in their tank.

Phallichthys amates, (the Merry Widow). The fish is a grey-olive colour, but has a pleasant black border to the dorsal and anal fins, from which it derives its name. This is an active little fish, peaceful, and eats all the usual foods. It is not so common as most live-bearers, but easy enough to reproduce.

Xiphophorus maculatus. Previously called *Platypoecillus maculatus*, and still endearingly referred to as Platys. These merry, peaceful little fish are deservedly popular. Somewhat short and stubby, they attain a length of, males 1¼″, females 1¾″. They will take any food, and are constantly nibbling at algae, thus helping to keep the plants in the tank clean. By line-breeding various colours have been produced – pure red, gold, black, blue, yellow with black fins, red with black fins; Sunset, a mixture of red, green and yellow; Festival, a mixture of black and green; Tuxedo, black with white shirt front, etc. etc.

There is also a closely related species, called *Platy variatus*. The males are richly coloured when adult. The dorsal is red and yellow, the belly red, yellow and green. The colours are bright and most attractive. Unfortunately, coloration does not appear until the fish is at least nine months old. Up till this time they are a drab grey-olive, and few people would give more than a shilling for them. However, mature specimens in colour can easily fetch 15/- each.

All platys are peaceful, and easy to reproduce.

Xiphophorus hellerii, (Swordtails). Though often recommended as a good fish for the beginner, the wisdom of this is doubted. These fishes grow quite large, males even reaching 5″ and females 5½″. They can then be spiteful, chivvying other fish; and although not actually doing them a great deal of damage, will harass them from morning to night. Through line-breeding the common green

C

Swordtail has been developed and there are now pure red Swords, red-eyed reds, golds, blacks; red with black fins; yellow with black fins etc. The males develop a long pointed extension in the lower rays of the caudal fins, and this pointed sword (which gives them their name) may attain a length of $2\frac{1}{4}''$. It is purely an adornment and is not used as a weapon, for the spines are softish and would bend before penetrating anything.

The males persistently pursue the females when they are not nibbling floating food from the surface, or algae growing on the walls and plants of the aquarium. Males when courting dart just as easily $3''$ or $4''$ backwards as they do $3''$ or $4''$ forwards. Their general shape is longer and thinner than the platy, and they are somewhat prone to eat their own and other fishes' babies. However, these and platys of solid hue give a contrast in colour that is bright and noticeable.

TEN

Egg-Laying Tropical Fishes

THERE ARE many more egg-laying tropicals than there are live-bearers. They do not all breed in the same way, therefore there can be no standard formula one can fit to egg-laying tropicals. Some families scatter fine adhesive eggs, the male chasing the female in and out amongst plant thickets; then taking a position side by side, they tremble together, pressing their vents towards each other. When the female is sufficiently excited she will let go six to twenty eggs. The male at the same time releases sperms into the water.

Each egg is enclosed in a moderately tough shell, but has a single microscopic hole through which one, and usually only one, spermatozoon enters. In spite of the fact that thousands of spermatozoa are free in the water, quite a few eggs will never become fertilised. These unfertile eggs, if not eaten by the parents or other fishes present, usually sink to the bottom and disintegrate.

Various eggs take different lengths of time to develop and hatch, some as quickly as eight hours, others as long as six months. The young fry of most of the smaller egg-laying tropicals when they first hatch out are so minute that they are barely 2 mms. long, and probably one-quarter of that thickness. Their chances of survival, therefore, in a community tank are practically nil. In the first twenty-four hours many of these fry are capable only of lying on the bottom or hanging on the plants of the aquarium, or tail downwards from plant leaves, attached by a slightly sticky thread on their heads. After a further twenty-four hours some are strong enough to make very short, jerky swimming movements which will carry them perhaps an inch or two before they rest on another leaf.

Most fry, when magnified, will be seen to have a rather swollen stomach. In actual fact this contains the yolk sac which is filled with food for them during their inert stage. But when this has been absorbed, and the fry has a little strength to move very short distances, it must obtain food elsewhere. The food most fry take first is called infusoria – minute organisms that are present in the air; these, upon finding water that contains fish excreta, rotting plant leaves etc., decide that this is a good medium in which to enter and breed. The infusoria breed rapidly under such conditions, and this is Nature's way of seeing that the fry do not starve to death. The fry are not strong enough to go in search of this food. It must be so thick in the water that it more or less goes to them. Here again, in a community tank the aquarist does not like to see the water so thick with infusoria that, although his baby fishes could feed readily, the water would not be clear enough to see the others. Even supposing all the conditions were right and the fry did manage to get sufficient food, as soon as they were capable of swimming easily about in the water they would be noticed by the bigger fishes and swallowed immediately. In a very, very thickly planted tank where there are only a few fishes it is possible that one or two fry might escape. They would probably take three weeks to reach the size of the normal newly-hatched live-bearer and, as stated before, newly-hatched live-bearers are likely to be eaten by all the other bigger fishes. Thus an egg-layer would have to survive a much longer period still.

Thus special egg-laying tropicals are bred in a separate tank, and only the male and female are placed in it. If in perfect condition, and given the right water and surroundings, they may spawn in the early morning on bright days. During the spawning period the parents are extremely excited and think of nothing else. As soon as spawning is over the male has lost a tremendous amount of spermatozoa and is thinner. The female has expelled 300 or more eggs, and is very much thinner. After their exertions both fishes are hungry, and both may spend the next few hours in eating up any eggs they can find. Thus the aquarist wishing to breed them removes the pair as soon as they cease to take an interest in each other and start searching for food. The eggs are left where they are. When the fry have reached the free-swimming stage they are fed with jars full of infusoria at the same temperature as the tank water.

When the fry are about a week old, added to the diet is newly-hatched brine shrimp. These are not the shrimps that human beings eat, but are tiny crustacea measuring about $\frac{1}{2}''$ when full grown. They are found in California and the Great Salt Lakes, where their eggs are collected and dried. These can be purchased in Pet Shops in small phials. Although they may have been dried from three weeks to ten years, when placed in a gallon of water to which has been added a heaped tablespoonful of salt, the eggs, which float, will hatch at a temperature of 78°F. in twenty-four to thirty-six hours. The tiny brine shrimps sink to the bottom where they can be seen hopping about in the lower strata of water. With a siphon tube the minute pink shrimps, each considerably smaller than a pin's head, can be siphoned off through very fine nylon material which strains the shrimps and allows the water to pass through. The pink mass then left in the nylon can be fed with the point of a penknife to the tiny fry in the breeding tanks.

In a further ten days the fry should have reached the size of newly-hatched live-bearers and, like those, can be given the foods previously mentioned, such as microworms, fine dried food and, later on, grindal worms. Once they have reached a length of $\frac{1}{2}''$ there is no reason why the aquarist should not raise them to maturity.

Other egg-laying fishes scatter adhesive eggs and these stick to the fronds of the feathery plants, some even to the side walls of the aquarium. They can be seen with the average magnifying-glass. They are not a bright silvery colour like the tiny air bubbles, but are slightly off-white and look as if they were pinheads of celluloid. Rearing fishes from these eggs follows the system given above.

The family *Anabantidae* build a bubble nest. Generally the male alone builds this nest. He takes bubbles of air, coats them with saliva and floats them to the surface, repeating the process until a small heaped mound of bubbles floats at, and above, the surface of the water. The male will then chase the female under this nest and, curving his body round hers, the two interlock like the crossing of two sickles. As they slowly sink through the water the male squeezes her firmly. She expels her eggs, which are fertilised by the sperms ejected by the male. Before the pair reach the bottom they break apart and pick up the slowly sinking eggs. Each is coated with a covering of air and saliva and blown into the nest.

Most males of this family are somewhat vicious, and if the female is not willing to co-operate they may chase her round the tank and tear her fins to pieces, sometimes killing her. So only ripe females full of eggs should be used when attempting to spawn these fishes. Even so, it is advisable to have her in a floating jar in the tank for safety, until the male has finished building his nest. Likewise after spawning, the male (who looks after the eggs and newly-hatched fry) will not trust the female in the vicinity and will drive her away. If the pair are in a small tank and the male cannot chase the female far enough away he gets the impression that she is refusing to go, and assumes that she is waiting to eat the eggs. Under these circumstances he may well kill her.

The *Anabantids* have an organ in their heads called the labyrinth. They come to the surface of the water, take a mouthful of atmospheric air, and store this in the labyrinth, slowly using this up as they swim about below the surface of the water. When it is all exhausted they come to the surface and take another gulp. These fishes are equipped with these organs because in their wild state they are usually found in rather dirty, muddy ponds and streams in hot sticky climates, where the water does not contain as much oxygen as in other localities. Thus they are not solely dependent on the oxygen dissolved in the water.

Another family of fishes are the mouth-breeders. Here male and female circle round each other just above the sand – in fact, they may make a small pit in the sand. The female releases a few eggs which the male immediately fertilises, and she then picks them up in her mouth. The circling dance continues, and when she has thirty to fifty eggs in her mouth the pair will separate. The female mouths the eggs, turning them over in her jaws, making sure that they receive fresh water, which enters her mouth and is expelled through her gills. In approximately twenty-eight days the eggs hatch. During this period she has not eaten, and will look somewhat wasted. Her belly is thin, but her jaws are now greatly extended. This is to provide the capacity for the newly-hatched fry inside.

When they are capable of swimming, and to a certain extent fending for themselves, she will open her mouth and allow the fry to swim out; but at the slightest disturbance the fry will rush back to her, scrambling to get inside this refuge provided by Nature. She scouts around for any others which have not seen the danger and scoops them in. She will keep them all safely tucked away until the danger is past, and maybe an hour or two later will allow them out again.

These fishes may be treated somewhat like live-bearers. The male has previously done his work, and therefore when the female is about to deliver her young no male need be present. With live-bearers the aquarist waits until the female's belly is deep, but with the mouth-breeders he waits until her belly is thin and her jaws well extended. She is transferred to a breeding tank, and when she has released the babies the aquarist must quickly net her out before the fry are able to regain the safety of her mouth. She is then returned to the stock tank and given a meal, and probably in another three weeks breeding will take place again. The fry are just a little smaller than live-bearers, but most will take micro-worms as first food, and after a few days they can go on to the normal fish diet previously mentioned.

The fishes most highly developed up the scale of evolution are the *Cichlids*. These fishes generally grow to 5" or more in length. A few mate for life, but the majority will spawn with any female filled with roe which, during the preliminary courtship, will not get frightened and run away. The pair will meet and grip each other's lips and a tussle ensues. If they are well matched mating is very likely to occur, but if either gives in too easily it may be pursued and killed by the other – presumably Nature's way of breeding from only the fittest specimens.

Once the pair have come to terms they will go in search of a spawning site. This may be a rock, a leaf in some cases, or a dip in the sand. They will clean the site thoroughly with their mouths. Some Cichlids will continue to dig away the sand, spitting it out a few inches away, until they have dug a pit which reaches the bottom of the aquarium and the base glass can be seen. Other Cichlids will clean a glass Bar, or a leaf, or rock, of every speck of algae growing upon it. Any other fishes which approach this selected spot too closely will be viciously attacked and rudely driven from the vicinity. If there are any plants near this site the mating pair consider that enemies may either be hiding in the thickets, or may approach unseen behind this cover; so, very wisely, they uproot it immediately. They now have a clear view all round. Of course the poor aquarist with a community tank soon has most of his plants ripped out, and to find the sand dug and mounded up is a most unpleasant sight. All of his other fishes will be huddled at one end of the tank, not daring to move an inch nearer to the aggressive pair. So it will be seen that the breeding of Cichlids in a community tank can make things very unpleasant for both the aquarist and the other fishes.

But to return to the would-be parents. Having cleaned the spot of every speck of algae, dust and dirt, the female deposits from her breeding tube (known as the ovipositor) a single adhesive egg which adheres to the rock. Moving slowly forward all the time by the use of her pectoral fins, the eggs follow each other out and thus form a single row. As she swims away the male goes over the line of eggs, ejecting spermatozoa over them. When he has reached the far end it is the female's turn to go in again and lay a second row of eggs. The turn and turn about continues until about 500-2,000 eggs are laid. As each fish reaches the end of the row of eggs it takes up guard duty whilst the other fish is laying or fertilising the eggs. If any other fish, smaller or larger than itself, approaches too closely it will be savagely attacked. Even a fish twice the size of the spawner will turn and flee before the determined onslaught. The intruder seems to realise that this fish is not just being pugnacious, but is prepared to fight for its young even at the cost of its own life. The interloper, having no such urge, ninety-nine times out of a hundred, gives ground.

Once the spawning is over the parents take it in turns to fan the eggs with their pectoral fins, ensuring in the same way as the mouth-breeder that there is a clean circulation of water over the eggs. Usually in about six days the eggs begin to hatch. At first just the wriggling tails appear, but soon the baby fishes struggle out of the eggs. They have sticky threads on their heads which attach them to the rock, plants or panes of glass, and of course during this period are absorbing the yolk sac. When they are about eighteen hours older some may be able to make struggling swimming strokes for an inch or two. But twenty-fours after this the whole mass are free swimming, and it is a most heartening sight to see a cloud of these tiny babies swimming and circling to and fro with the proud parents gliding around them, now more viciously determined than ever to prevent any intruder from snatching even a single fry.

During the latter days of this period the parents are very thorough about cleanliness, and if the breeding site with its discarded eggshells begins to look dirty and untidy, they will pick the babies up in their mouths and transfer them to a newly dug pit elsewhere in the aquarium. Each is mouthed over and washed in transit, one parent guarding those that have been moved, and the other those still awaiting removal.

The babies must be fed infusoria for the first few days, after which brine shrimp may be added to their diet. In ten days to a fortnight they can go on to microworms. However, the parents will continue to care for the young until they are half-grown. Occasionally one or other desires to spawn again, and if they consider their home too crowded they may in a few hours swallow every one of the smaller babies. So the aquarist wishing to raise young Cichlids is well advised to remove the parents once the babies are $\frac{1}{4}''$ long. They are then large enough to do without parental care, providing no other fishes or other enemies are introduced to gobble them up.

Some of the family *Cyprinodontidae* will spawn in nylon mops. These are mops made from 100% nylon wool which will not disintegrate in water. They prefer soft peaty water and the eggs, which are roughly the size of a pin's head (but, according to species, may be slightly larger or smaller) can be seen among the strands of the mops. If one or two strands are picked up, and the thumb and forefinger slid along, many eggs which have passed unnoticed can be felt. They have such a tough shell that they can be picked off and dropped into a plastic sandwich box filled with the same water. The sandwich box then has its lid put on and can be kept separately, provided the temperature is the same; or, failing this, floated back in the breeding tank.

Some eggs are added daily, and after fourteen days the first will begin to hatch. The fry are fed on infusoria and brine shrimp. Any more eggs discovered are placed in a second sandwich box, for it must be remembered that by the time the second lot hatch in a further fourteen days, the first box will now be full of tiny fishes and these would, sooner or later, devour the smaller second batch if they were together.

Some species of this family are called annual fishes. This is because they live in ponds in East Africa from which, during the dry season, all the water evaporates. The parents have spawned in the dead leaves and rotted rushes which were growing in the pond and have now formed a compost on the bottom. Of course when all the water has evaporated the parents are left stranded.

They soon die, or are seized by birds to be swallowed in a merciful release. The pond may remain dry, and the mud and compost at the bottom will get brittle and crack under the fiercely blazing sun. It may stay like this for as long as three to four months, but eventually the rainy season comes again. Torrential rains pour from the skies. At first little trickles run into the holes, but soon streams are flowing into these depressions and the ponds are once again reformed.

Now the dormant eggs, which have remained so long dry, feel the touch of water. The shells are slightly softened by it, the masses of infusoria present may even bite at the shells of the eggs. Sooner or later the shells give way and the tiny fish emerge. The dry vegetation in the water makes a fine medium for the infusoria to multiply, so food is abundant. The young fishes take their fill, and grow rapidly. They must grow rapidly, for they have to mature, breed and die by the next dry season; but sufficient survive this ordeal, and the cycle of life continues for another year.

To breed these fishes at home, therefore, the base of the tank is lined with waterlogged peat to a depth of 1″ or more. The parents dive into it together and spawn, and the spawning continues over a period of perhaps a month. The aquarist does not have to be quite so cruel as Nature, and when the fishes have been in a month the parents are removed. They may be transferred to another breeding tank, or replaced in the stock tank, but the water in the breeding tank is then siphoned off. The eggs remain behind in the peat at the bottom; it will, of course, still be very damp but in a centrally heated aquarium, or removed to an airing cupboard, the dampness will slowly evaporate, and in a month or two will be bone dry.

Some species must remain dry for a month, some two, some three; but eventually peaty water containing an abundant supply of infusoria is poured on to the dried peat. In a few hours the peat becomes sodden, and much of it begins to sink. In the clear brown water will be seen a few tiny fry. The first will appear within a few hours, others may take several days. Possibly this is because they were not all laid at the same period, possibly some are lodged in a nodule of peat that has not yet become soaked right through. Once the fry are fully hatched brine shrimp is added to the diet as well as infusoria, and, in about another week to ten days, microworms. These fishes are not very keen on dried foods, and so not too much of this should be provided. They much prefer live or frozen foods, as described in Chapter 4.

There are of course many other species which differ somewhat from these general descriptions, but this book is not large enough to cover all these. Nevertheless what has been written describes a great many species in the four or five families, and should be a good guide to what to expect. This book cannot either list or illustrate the thousands of species of egg-layers found throughout the world; but below is an alphabetical list of egg-laying fishes which will get on well together in a community tank. The beginner will want to know what the species are, and gain an impression of what they look like, together with points for their care and maintenance.

Acanthophthalmus semicinctus, (Kuhli eel). Family: Cobitidae. These harmless little fishes are excellent scavengers. In shape they resemble miniature snakes. They do not have scales, and are covered with a skin, coloured a chocolate brown in patches like a row of saddles the entire length of the fish. Between the blotches the skin is a pale pink colour. The species has small barbels or whiskers about its mouth, and with these sensitive feelers it is able to detect all things edible, even when they are slightly below the top level of the sand. It will dig them out and swallow them. Male and female similar. Breeding difficult.

Ambasis lala (Glass fish). Family Ambassidae. These very transparent fish attain a length of 1″ to 1¼″. Males have a golden sheen over the body, and the fins are edged with electric blue. Very peaceful. Eats most foods, but prefers live food. A breeding pair will spawn freely, but any two picked out by the aquarist will not necessarily oblige.

Aphyocharax rubripinnis (Blood fins). Family Characidae. Pleasing little fish which grow to about 1½″ in length. The body is a pale greeny-blue, all the fins being bright red; but when not in a condition to its liking, or when chivvied by other fishes, the fins are apt to pale. A ready spawner, but the eggs are not so easy to hatch. The fish will take any food, and is peaceful.

Aphyosemion australe (Lyre tail). Family Cyprinodontidae. The genus *Aphyosemion* contains some beautiful species, and although this is one of the commonest it still ranks as one of the loveliest. Normally the male carries the colour. The female is a pale brown, covered with reddish spots. She attains a length of 2″, and he reaches 2¼″. His body is a rosy-brown colour, the fore part of the flanks a silvery-blue covered with red spots. The ventral fins are very far forward, and are bright orange-red edged with black. The dorsal, which is far back on the body, is red-brown. Above this is a band of chocolate, and the outer edge is a silvery-blue. The tip may be white or bright yellow. The anal fin, which is somewhat long and pointed in the male (but rounded in the female) bears the same colours as the dorsal fin.

His tail is magnificent. It is shaped like a musical lyre, with a small sword top and bottom, hence the name. It is divided into three portions, the upper and lower being bright yellow, pale blue, and ending in white or golden tips. The centre portion is blue over-speckled with red spots, and has a chocolate-maroon edging.

The fish is very peaceful, and will take most foods, even dried food. It prefers soft peaty water. May be bred in a small battery jar, for the species does not require a great deal of oxygen. In the battery jar place some brown peaty water and a nylon mop. Place the pair (or, preferably, one male and two females) in this, which should be at a temperature of 72°F. Within a few hours they will be spawning. The light golden eggs, the size of a pin's head, may be seen amongst the strands of the mop. These can be picked off daily with the fingers and placed in a plastic sandwich box containing some soft water at the same temperature. In fourteen days the eggs start to hatch. Usually the parents will not have finished spawning, so any further eggs are placed in a second sandwich box.

The young should be fed with infusoria, and a few days later on with newly-hatched brine shrimp, when they will grow rapidly. The parents may continue to spawn until the aquarist has six or more sandwich boxes of eggs or fry in various stages of development.

A. australe does not usually appreciate life in a community tank. First of all, the water is probably too hard, and secondly, it does not like being buffeted by other fishes. It spends much time stationary in the water with just the fins and tail quivering slightly, making small darts every now and then to catch a small piece of food. In a community tank it is rarely able to lead this quiet life, and often dies prematurely.

Apistogramma ramirezi. One of the dwarf Cichlids, often known as the Mauve Cichlid, is a colourful, peaceful little fish which grows to only $2\frac{1}{2}''$-$2\frac{3}{4}''$. The main colour is a beautiful mauvy to purplish blue with a rosy colour near the belly, and sometimes suffusing here and there throughout the scales. The fish does not like being buffeted about by bigger fishes. It is quite easy to spawn, generally selecting the inside of a flower-pot laid on its side on the sand. It is not over fond of dried food.

Barbus gelius (Miniature barb). Family Cyprinidae. A pretty little golden barb, reaching only $1\frac{1}{4}''$-$1\frac{1}{2}''$ in length. The general body colour is gold but blackish blotches appear over the body. Females are deeper bellied than males, and the species is easy to breed. They are not in the least aggressive, but are quite capable of looking after themselves with fishes that are not more than double their size. They will take any food, and nearly always look bright and perky.

Barbus nigrofasciatus, (Ruby barb). Family Cyprinidae. One of the most popular fishes kept in aquaria, and an old favourite. It grows to a length of $1\frac{3}{4}''$-$2''$. When immature, both male and female have three broad vertical bars of black on a silvery background. Sexes can be told apart, even when quite young, as the male's dorsal fin is a solid black. The female's dorsal is clear along it's upper edge. When adult, males may turn a fiery red from the nose to the middle bar, and jet black from there to the tail, all the fins then being solid black. Strangely enough, males do not usually present their best colours when females are present in the tank; so those aquarists not wishing to breed will find that two males will make a much better display. Eats any food, easy to breed, and is not aggressive.

Barbus oligolepsis, (Chequer barb). Family Cyprinidae. Another small barb of $1\frac{1}{4}''$-$1\frac{1}{2}''$ in length. The overall colour is a golden brown, sometimes turning a rusty red. The scales are coloured alternately, from which its common name is derived. If one can imagine rows of bricks of different heights laid alternately, the right impression of the chequering can be obtained. The fins of the female are mostly clear, but those of the male are a deep orange edged with black. The fish is easy to feed, peaceful, and will take any food.

Barbus titteya, (Cherry barb). Family Cyprinidae. $1\frac{1}{2}''$-$1\frac{3}{4}''$. One of the smaller barbs, which is peaceful, will take any food, and seems to enjoy life in the aquarium. When young it is a pale brown colour with a dark brown stripe running from nose to tail. In some lights this stripe has a golden hue on its upper side. When mature, males turn a coppery brown, occasionally with a reddish tinge, hence the name. The fins are slightly round, and when courting the male spreads and displays these to perfection in front of the female. For spawning it prefers soft water, the young being easy to raise.

Brachydanio albolineatus, (Pearl danio). Family Rasborinae. These hardy fishes are extremely active, swimming mostly in the upper strata of the water and continually on the go. The body colour is a mother-of-pearl, but this shows better in daylight than electric light. They are shoal fishes, and usually follow each other about. It is one of the fishes recommended for a species tank, as a shoal is more noticeable, whereas in a community tank this effect is lost. It is very peaceful, eats any food, and is easy to breed, though inclined to eat its own eggs.

Brachydanio nigrofasciatus, (Spotted danio). Family Rasborinae. This is probably the smallest of the three species, and a little less common. The body is a pale gold; a deep blue stripe runs from the gill plate to the tail, the upper edge shining gold. The lower rear portion of the body and anal fin is spotted. In other respects similar to the above.

Brachydanio rerio, (Zebra danio). Family Rasborinae. This active little fish is usually seen in most community tanks. It reaches $1\frac{1}{2}''$-$1\frac{3}{4}''$, females being slightly larger than males. The body is a beautiful silver crossed by several horizontal stripes of deep blue. These stripes are also present in the tail fin. Sexing with all danios is simple, as the female is much deeper bellied.

They are easy to spawn, but are inclined to eat their own eggs. Stainless steel mesh traps are recommended to prevent this.

Cheirodon axelrodi, (Cardinal tetra). Family Characidae. Originally called *Hyphessobrycon cardinalis*, this fish is similar to the Neon tetra, but grows slightly larger and is even more brilliant. It prefers soft peaty water. The striking feature of this fish is the brilliant blue-green lines that passes through the eyes, the length of the body to the tail. Above this the back is a rusty olive, and beneath the blue line the body is a brilliant red, though there is a thin white line under the belly. This highly colourful, peaceful fish is a gem of the aquarium. Many imagine from the brilliance that it must be luminous. Actually in the dark the fish is not more easy to see than any other. Males reach a length of $1\frac{1}{4}''$, females $1\frac{1}{2}''$ and she is deeper bellied.

The fishes spawn after the fashion of neons, but the eggs will not hatch unless the water is extremely soft. The babies are exceedingly small, but hardy. The author raised a first spawn of eighty-six to maturity without any difficulty. The fish will take most small foods, fresh or live, and will take some dried food, but is not quite so fond of this as are neons. The species seems more difficult to induce to spawn than neons.

Colisa lalia, (Dwarf gourami). Family Anabantidae. This beautiful little fish is peaceful and easy to feed, and since it is a labyrinth and takes air from the atmosphere it will stand a fair amount of overcrowding. The male is beautiful. The body is brilliantly coloured with thin red and blue vertical stripes, and there is a big blue patch on the gill plate. All his fins are red, speckled with bright blue.

The female carries the same pattern, but at first glance looks a plain silver. On closer examination it will be seen that she does actually carry the red and blue stripes, but so much fainter that they can be seen only in certain lights.

It will take any food, and does not molest other fishes; in fact, it is somewhat shy and is apt to hide its beauty behind the plants. It breeds readily, but after the eggs are in the bubble nest it is as well to remove the female. The babies are extremely small, and to rear them all is difficult. Quite a few may die off when they reach the age of about three weeks.

Corydoras aeneus, (Bronze catfish). Family Siluroidea. It is advisable to have at least one catfish in every community tank, as these are the scavengers. With their whiskery mouths they will search out any particle of food left uneaten by the other fishes, even digging down into the sand $\frac{1}{4}$" to reach a titbit. This grubbing habit of theirs also serves to keep the surface of the sand loose, which without a catfish present may sometimes become sticky and rather compacted. The fishes dash up to the surface for a mouthful of air and down again to the bottom, but apart from these occasional dashes most of their lives are spent on the sand.

Although they grow to a length of $2\frac{1}{2}$" they are absolutely peaceful and never attack any other fish, even at breeding time. Perhaps the knowledge that they are covered with hard scales and bony plates gives them the confidence that they are armour-protected, and thus there is no need to bother about driving off other fishes which might otherwise attack them.

The colour of this species is a golden-green, and shows an arrow-head pattern along the flanks. When breeding, the female takes the sperms from the male in her mouth, cleaning a leaf or the glass wall of the aquarium free of algae, and drops a few eggs into a cup temporarily made by her ventral fins. She then spits the sperm on to the leaf and immediately presses the eggs on to the spot where they adhere very firmly. The process is repeated until 600-800 eggs are deposited. The young hatch in five to six days. Although most catfishes are not difficult to breed, the impression remains that they are practically unbreedable.

Corydoras julii, (Leopard catfish). Another species of this large genus, though not quite so common. The body and fins are covered in large black spots on a silver ground. This makes it most striking and one of the prettiest of the catfishes. In all other respects it is similar to the foregoing species.

Corydoras paleatus, (Mottled catfish). Probably the commonest of all species seen in aquaria, though *C. aeneus* runs it a close second. The body is greenish, mottled with dark patches of blue-green. It is just as good a scavenger as the other species, but because it is not so rare may be a little cheaper.

Epiplatys chaperi, (Red-throated Panchax). Family Cyprino-dontidae. One of the smaller Panchax, this attractive little fish is a greeny-gold colour over the body. Four or five rather widely spaced bars cross the flanks vertically, although these are more pronounced in the lower half of the body and in the rear portion. Males grow to a length of $1\frac{3}{4}''$, females $1\frac{1}{2}''$. The bottom edge of the male's anal fin is jet black, so are the lower rays of his tail, and this protrudes in a very short sword. The female's fins are clear.

The fish usually occupies a space just below the surface of the water. Each has a rudimentary eye on the crown of the head, and although it cannot see with this organ it will instantly detect any shadow passing overhead and dive for protection.

This is one of the species that should be spawned in nylon mops, and the rather small eggs taken off by thumb and fore-finger and hatched in a plastic sandwich box. It prefers live food, but will take tiny pieces of shrimp, crab, meat, and some floating dried food.

Gyrinocheilus aymonieri, (Sucking loach). Though there are several algae-eating fish, this rather recent importation seems to be best of all at this cleaning job. The fish grows to $3''$ in length, but it is absolutely peaceful. In fact, it has no teeth with which to attack.

The body is elongated and blotched with several small bars, but these do not entirely cross the body. The groundwork is a brownish-yellow, but the belly is white.

The fish is remarkable for two reasons. (i) It has no swim bladder. (ii) It breathes differently from others. Whilst most fishes breathe in through the mouth and exhale through the gills, this species has a supplementary opening just above the gills for inhaling.

The fins are large; these are necessary because, having no swim bladder, it is unable to lie in mid-water without any effort and sinks to the bottom. It makes short darts through the water by using its comparatively large fins. Immediately it stops using these fins it will sink again. However, it overcomes some of its diffi-culties by having sucker lips, and can quickly attach itself to any plant leaf or the walls of the aquarium.

Its food consists mainly of algae, and several will clear a large tank of this weedish plant in next to no time. But once the algae is cleared, unless more is growing all the time the fish will appreciate chopped lettuce or spinach. It will also scavenge dried food from the sand.

Hyphessobrycon callistus minor, (Minor tetra). Family Characidae. This somewhat diamond-shaped fish is a beautiful deep red. The dorsal has a black portion in the upper half tipped with white, as do the rays of the anal fin, but a black border edges this fin, the rear point being a solid black. It grows to a length of $1\frac{1}{4}''$, though females are slightly larger. They are also deeper bellied. Although it somewhat resembles the following species, the difference is that this one has a black dot in the region of the shoulder and is a brighter glowing red. It prefers soft water, and with these conditions is not difficult to breed. It will take any food, but has the habit of occasionally nipping the edges of other fishes' fins.

Hyphessobrycon callistus serpae, (Serpae tetra). Family Characidae. Similar in all respects to the foregoing, except that it is a blacker red and there is a small black stripe, instead of a spot, in the shoulder region.

Hyphessobrycon innesi, (Neon tetra). Family Characidae. Until the introduction of the Cardinal tetra this beautiful little fish was considered the most brilliant. It reaches a length of only, males $1\frac{1}{8}''$, females $1\frac{1}{4}''$. The body is traversed horizontally by a startling, brilliant blue-green line, but where this line passes below the dorsal fin there is a definite upward kink in it. Below the line in the rear portion of the body the fish is bright red, the forepart of the belly pure white. The fish is peaceful and will take any food.

For years the species was considered most difficult, if not impossible, to breed in captivity, but the author now finds it one of the easiest species to reproduce. Any male and any plump female are chosen and placed in the breeding tank in the late afternoon. The breeding tank contains merely soft peaty water, where the total hardness does not exceed ten parts per million. In the water is placed a nylon mop. Invariably the pair spawn the following morning, and although the eggs are difficult to see in the mop, a glass-bottomed tank is used and many can be seen lying on the floor of the tank when viewed from underneath.

In very bright weather the eggs will hatch in as short a period as six hours, and even in dull weather they will be hatched in twenty-four hours. The fry are extremely small, but can be seen moving about on the bottom of the tank when viewed from underneath. They are given infusoria for the first three days, and then some brine shrimp is added to the diet. Although the young fish are generally not seen for nearly ten days, feeding continues. In three weeks the start of the blue line can be seen above each eye. The average spawn raised amounts to eighty, although the spawn consists usually of over 130 eggs. If a few babies are separated out, given extra room and extra food, they will grow at such a pace that they are breedable within twelve weeks from the egg. This shows that, when conditions are right, a fish considered to be unbreedable can prove to be one of the easiest of all. The author without exaggeration considers, after breeding thousands of neons, that they are much easier than the Zebra danio, which in the past was recommended as the easiest fish for beginners to breed.

To back this statement, consider that the neon egg is vulnerable for only twenty-four hours at most, whereas the Zebra danio takes five or more days to hatch, and during this period when it cannot in any way protect itself it is liable to be attacked by infusoria, bacteria, and the chemicals in the water.

The Neon tetra will take any food, and is quite happy with a good dried food.

Hyphessobrycon pulchripinnis, (Lemon tetra). Family Characidae. Reaching a length of approximately 1¾″, this pleasing fish is peaceful and attractive. The body is a pale yellow, the upper portion of the eye a bright red, whilst the dorsal and anal fins are striped with yellow in the leading rays and edged with black. It will take any food, is sprightly and always on the go. It looks best in soft peaty water, and breeds easily in this.

Hyphessobrycon roseaceus, (Rosy tetra). Family Characidae. Rather deep bodied, this fish under the right conditions is a bright rosy red. The dorsal of the male is elongated and arches over the back towards the tail in a long point, the upper portion being jet black. The ventral fins are bright red, tipped with white, and the first rays of his anal fin are the same, but the trailing edge of this fin has a black border.

The female is similar in colour but she is deeper bodied, and the upper tip of her dorsal fin is edged with white but finished with a red tip.

It prefers soft water. More difficult to induce to spawn than most Characins, but a couple once spawned will continue to spawn freely. Will take any food and is peaceful.

Nannostomus anomalus, (Pencil fish). Family Characidae. This is a smart little fish with quick jerky movements. Often it appears to have a dark horizontal stripe running from eye to tail, over a brownish body. However, the tips of the ventral fins are edged with electric blue. Kept in soft peaty water, the male is very lively. He then turns a coppery colour and his fins can be a fiery red, offset as usual by the electric blue tips. The species is very peaceful. Having a small mouth, it will take any food small enough to swallow. It spawns readily amongst floating plants, and will spawn over a period of a week. Usually a pair put in a breeding tank should be left alone, and removed after seven days. Shortly after eggs will begin to hatch. The young are small and must be fed fine infusoria at first.

Otocinclus affinis, (Sucking catfish). Family Siluroidea. Another of the algae cleaners. It grows to a length of 1¾″, and has sucker lips. It is peaceful. It attaches itself to plants and the walls of the aquarium, devouring algae that is either growing or floating. The fish is an elongated tubular shape, the colour being brownish-grey, but it has dark mottled markings over the body and fins. Unfortunately it is not always hardy. Although at times imported in thousands, the majority are dead within a few weeks.

Pristella riddlei, (X-ray fish). Family Characidae. When this fish was first introduced to aquaria it was nicknamed the X-ray fish as the hind portion of the body is almost clear, the backbone showing clearly when a bright light is behind the tank. However, the *Ambasis lala* is really much more transparent, because *P. riddlei's* internal organs are encased in an opaque silvery sac. It is only 1¼″-1½″ long. The body is silver, but the dorsal and anal fins have yellow rays cut off by a black spot and finished with a white tip. The tail is bright red. It is a harmless little fish, always active and will take any food.

Pterophyllum eimekei, (Angel fish). Family Cichlidae. Even the uninitiated who do not keep tropical fishes have seen so many drawings and pictures of the angel fish that it is known to all. There are actually three different species, but this is the one most generally seen. The body is round and disc-shaped. An angel seen from the side view will appear a big fish, but seen head on it is little more than a straight line. The huge dorsal and anal fins resemble wings, hence the name. Though a Cichlid, it is not usually pugnacious, though it can be temperamental. Some occasionally mope, refuse to eat, and die, but the majority are happy.

It spawns like other Cichlids, except that the eggs are deposited on a bar stood upright in the aquarium, or a tall narrow leaf of some large plant. The parents tend the eggs and newly-hatched fry but many will eat their own young after a few days. Best remove the bar or leaf, and hatch the eggs in a separate breeding tank. They must be aerated during the incubation period to imitate the fanning action the parents provide with their pectoral fins to ensure a steady flow of clean water over the eggs, which prevents bacteria settling upon them and puncturing them.

Many aquarists are under the impression that angel fish will not eat dried food. If a good dried food is used they not only eat it, but often prefer it.

Through line-breeding one is able to purchase (1) the ordinary angel fish, which has a silvery body traversed vertically from tip of dorsal fin to tip of anal fin, across the body and tail, by several black bars. (2) Black lace angel, which is darker, and the black bars so prominent and flecked with spots that it resembles a piece of black lace held up to a light. (3) The pure black angel, which should be a solid black all over.

Rasbora heteromorpha, (Harlequin). Family Rasborinae. This is a striking little fish of 1½″ length. The body is a suffused pinkish gold, but a beautiful dark blue to black triangle adorns the rear portion of the flanks. The fish should be deep bodied and males will show much more red in the dorsal fin and in the caudal peduncle above the apex of the triangle. Females are rounder and more golden. Many consider this fish to be difficult to sex, but a careful comparison will show the difference. It prefers soft water and is not one of the easiest Rasboras to spawn. When this occurs the female will turn upside down under a leaf and deposit her eggs on the underside. The male follows, and rolling over fertilises her egg, the process continuing for roughly an hour, after which the parents should be removed, as they are inclined to eat the eggs or any fry that hatch. The fish is extremely peaceful, will take any food. It prefers to be with fishes of its own size that will not buffet and harass it. A shoal of these fishes is a delight to watch.

Rasbora pauciperforata, (Glowlight Rasbora). Family Rasborinae. Most of the Rasboras prefer soft water and only show their best colours under such conditions. This species has a narrow elongated shape, and the body is a rusty brown. From the tip of the nose to the tail runs a red line. Under conditions to its liking the fish takes on a fiery glow, and the red lines becomes so brilliant that it looks almost fluorescent. The species is peaceful and will take any food. It is rather difficult to breed.

Tanichthys albonubes, (White Cloud Mountain minnow). Family Rasborinae. A close relation of the Rasboras, this pretty fish was discovered in the water from the melted snow of the White Cloud Mountain in China; not of course at the point where it just melts, but lower down in the area where it reaches a temperature of 70°F. It will therefore stand moderately low temperatures. It is a typical shoal fish, and looks best when swimming with a number of its own kind. When young the fish has a beautiful blue-green line running from nose to tail along the body. Below this there is a broader bright red line which runs from the nose right through to the end of the tail. The back is olive, the belly silver. The dorsal and anal fins are red, tipped with white. Males reach 1¼″, females 1½″, but at this size the green line tends to fade, and is nothing like so brilliant. Baby White Clouds less than ¼″ long are actually brighter than neons of this size, but unlike the neon the vivid coloration does not persist all its life. It is extremely peaceful, will take any food, and is one of the easiest aquarium fishes to breed.

Thayeria sanctemaria, (Penquin). Family Characidae. Though not brilliant in colour, this is a very striking fish. The body is a beautiful silver, but an intense black stripe runs from the gill plate along the length of the body, and then takes a downward sweep through the centre of the lower lobe of the tail. The fish grows to a length of $2\frac{1}{2}''$-$2\frac{3}{4}''$, and the only difference in sex is that the female is slightly deeper bodied and her belly is a little more rounded. It has a habit of staying in one spot in mid-water, the tail slowly dropping; as soon as it reaches an angle of 15° off horizontal it flicks the tail up again. This flicking movement is continuous all its life. At intervals it makes short darts, only to pause again, and repeat the jerky movement. When trying to catch it the fish is very streamlined and a swift swimmer.

It will take any food and, once induced to spawn, will breed regularly. A few specimens occasionally acquire the bad habit of taking a sly nip now and again at other fishes' fins.

Trichogaster leeri, (Lace gourami). Family Anabantidae. Though the species grows to 5" in length it is very peaceful. When young, both sexes are a silvery colour, and the body and fins are covered with small circles as though encased in lace or network. Adult males develop an orange throat and breast and the feelers or ventral fins carry the same hue. The male's dorsal fin grows larger and much more pointed than the female's. Like other labyrinth fishes they surface frequently to gulp atmospheric air, and when breeding build a bubble nest intermingled with pieces of plant. Will take any food.

ELEVEN

Fish Houses

MANY AQUARISTS starting with one tank soon become so absorbed with the keeping of tropical fish that they acquire a breeding tank. They soon find that they need a 'growing on' tank; then wish to spawn a second or third species, and before they know what is happening they have five or six tanks; and still they need more. To have such a number in the average room soon becomes overpowering, and it is not surprising if his wife raises objections, particularly if, in order to feed his baby fishes, the aquarist also keeps cultures of infusoria (which at best do not smell too sweetly), as well as hatchings of brine shrimps in jars of salt water, to say nothing of cultures of microworms, grindal worms etc. in flat wooden boxes.

To cope with this the budding fish-breeder really requires a fish house in the garden. Quite a small shed will do, a staging of wood is put up, roughly 3″ × 2″ thick, or of angle-iron, on which the tanks will stand in tiers. The roof should be of glass, and lined with polythene sheeting to retain heat. Probably during a dry summer a blind will be necessary to prevent sunlight from providing too much heat and illumination. The walls of the shed should be preferably double with a 3″-5″ cavity between them, so that heat is retained as much as possible. The interior in winter will probably have to be heated. Space heating is the cheapest form. This may be achieved by a boiler burning solid fuel, gas or electricity, or even by paraffin heaters. The last-named are inclined to give off an oily smoke which necessitates cleaning the surface of the water regularly.

The floor space below the tanks should be of concrete so that the spilling of water does not matter, and on it of course all the various food cultures can be kept.

Without space heating it is of course necessary to have heaters or thermostats in the tanks, but in breeding some of the fishes these items can be rather a nuisance, for a female may hide herself behind a thermostat and the ardent male is unable to drive her out. When these encumbrances are missing the male can keep driving the female until he excites her sufficiently to spawn.

It must be pointed out that the beginner will not make a fortune out of breeding fishes, but he should get endless interest and amusement from it, and at least be able to sell sufficient fishes to cover the cost of his hobby, and possibly make a small amount extra to purchase further equipment. He must not be too disappointed if the first attempts at breeding fail. Try again. One cannot become an expert in a few months. Some of the leading breeders have thirty years or more of experience behind them. Keep notes about the water, temperature, conditions etc., and do not repeat the same mistake over and over again. No matter what information one can get from others or from literature, there is nothing so good as first-hand experience. Every day more confidence will be gained, and eventually past experiments will provide knowledge and skill.

It is perhaps consoling to remember that the expert breeders, well-known throughout the world to-day, had originally to breed their first fish. Who knows, perhaps the reader may eventually become the greatest authority of all time on this subject.

Index